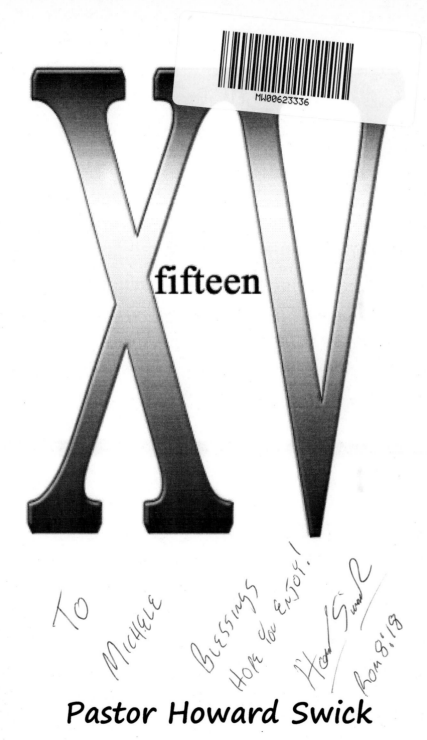

XV

fifteen

Pastor Howard Swick

To MICHELE

Blessings
Hope you enjoy!

Howard Swick

Rom 8:18

XV fifteen

Printed in the United States of America.

ISBN: 978-1-930672-72-7

All Scripture quotations are from the *King James Version* of the Bible unless otherwise noted.

For more information, write:
Pastor Howard Swick
PO Box 886
Philippi, WV 26416
Phone - 304-823-3428

DEDICATION

First, I would like to dedicate this book to my God and my Lord and Savior Jesus Christ! The Love of my God is unconditional, even for a sinner such as I.

To the Love of my life Benita; you are my soul mate. Without Benita - Howard doesn't exist!

To the Gifts of my life, Hannah and Kaitie; no one could ever love their daughters any more than your daddy loves you!

To my beloved family at Haven of Hope Worship Center; I count it a blessing to serve as your Pastor.

To all of my family, friends, and work peers; thank you for the encouragement.

Pastor Howard Swick

TABLE OF CONTENTS

Foreword
Recommendations
To The Reader
The Vision
Preface

1. Destiny 19
2. My Joy-Maker -- "Mini Me" 21
3. An Angel Named Kaitie 25
4. Time Stood Still & A Nation Prayed! 33
5. I'm An Army Of One 37
6. Who's Your JESUS? 43
7. Fellowship 47
8. Walkin' On Your Own Two Legs! 51
9. The Tribe & The Sticks!!! 55
10. Giving It Up To A Stranger 59
11. Soak In God's River 63
12. Mission 3:16 67
13. Prayer 69
14. SHINE 75
15. Youth Attack "It's Time To Fight Back!!" ... 77
16. Sin 81
17. 7 Ways To Praise & Worship 85
18. The BIBLE 89
19. Blessed Times Two 95
20. Christmas - Just Another Day? 97
21. GIVE UP? 99
22. The Walk 101
23. Her Daddy 103
24. Joy 105
25. Spiritual Lamb 107
26. Starfish 111

27. Say What? 113

28. The One 115

29. Healing Rain 117

30. Local Church 121

31. Faith Lifestyle 123

32. Patience vs. Impatience.................... 125

33. The Book Of James 129

34. Why Not Here? 133

35. Commitment 139

36. National Day Of Prayer 141

37. Ministry 145

38. Mothers 149

39. Apostolic Oversight 151

40. Divided We Fall / United We Stand 155

41. A Story Of 1 Man / 2 Kings 161

42. He Didn't Like Preachers 167

43. The Love Of Her Life 171

44. That's One Great Dad! 175

45. The Earth Is The Lord's? 179

46. Tammy Faye 183

47. Follow The Yellow Brick Road?.................. 187

48. A Father & His Son 195

49. Green Eggs & Ham Evangelism 197

50. The Fish Lady &
    A Stranger On The Other Line 201

51. A Love Song Without Words 205

52. Light Up A Life................................ 207

53. My Friend R.P. 209

54. A Call From Ric 213

55. My Benita & Meat Loaf? 217

56. March 11th 219

57. That's Where I Came From.................... 223

58. Camp Chaos.................................... 227

59. I Lay Down 231

60. ME 233

FOREWORD

I am not a great believer in long, protracted forewords. I mean, if you want to hear from me, you should buy one of my books. This is not about me or my analysis of what has been written here. This is about Howard, Benita and the girls. That's what's so cool about it. It really is about them and the Jesus that they know and serve.

Fifteen years of notes, blogs, songs, poems, sermons and stories. The tale of a young man and his family as they navigate through these minefields called life and ministry. These are real people, doing real things to love and serve a real Lord, His real people and each other for real!

There are lots of reasons to love "Howie" and "Ben":

- They have great kids.
- They have a great church full of wonderful people.
- They are young and enthusiastic.

- They make great music together.
- They are fun to "hang" with.
- They know a GREAT Chinese restaurant!

The best thing, however, is that their smiles are never far away. No matter what, those big ol' grins are just around the corner with the laughs right behind. I've always said, "Never trust religious leaders that don't know how to laugh, especially at themselves."

I love that this book is not contrived. I like that it's taken Howard 15 years to do and is not slapped together as a quick grab for a buck. I'm grateful it comes from the heart.

I remember when random was not a bad thing. I hear the kids say, "How Random!" now days and it doesn't sound good at all. But quilts are made up of random pieces and there is hardly anything more cozy and comforting than a well made (hand made) quilt. The more random the pieces the more colorful the quilt! So here we are with 15 years of bits and pieces to keep us warm. How cool (warm?) is that?

Howard and Benita have character. In a world full of bland, colorless half-heartedness, character is wonderful to find. It makes them shine … ear to ear!

This is not just a load of hype form people that have never been through anything. It's more like rainbows during the storm. It's staying faithful to a vision and a promise and each other in spite of everything. That's the stuff that REAL stories are made of.

The mountains of West Virginia are a backdrop hard to beat. The cast of characters is formed as much by their environment as anything. Praising God in high places takes on a whole new meaning as you drive along US 250 from Elkins to Philippi on a cold November morning. A small town in the hills makes for a special kind of people. It has been these folks that have called the Swicks "Pastor".

I'm glad to know Pastor "H" and Pastor "B". Having them for friends enriches my life. I pray that reading this book will enrich yours, as well. Traversing the terrain of the heart is always exciting. Be blessed as you make the trip.

Grace and Peace,

Mike Warnke
Celebrations of Hope, Inc.
Ponte Vedra Beach, Florida
September 5th, 2009

RECOMMENDATIONS

Pastor Howard "Howie" is one of a select few people that you meet in life that brightens everyone he comes in contact with. I thank God for sharing Howie with me and my family. His spin on life and spirituality is a refreshing, honest approach that he lives by and makes everyone he comes in contact with a better person.

- Ric Cooper
General Manager/Owner of WQLV-FM
President *Upod L.L.C.*

Pastor Swick is a man who demonstrates the highest level of character, a caring attitude and a commitment to serving people in need. His integrity is unquestioned and this part of his character is worn on his sleeve. Truthfulness and honesty are cornerstones of his very being and that is what brings many to know that the trust can be counted on. He is the Shepherd of his flock at his church and is always available for counseling or just a caring ear for those who want to share. His caring attitude is recognized by the community as well as his church. He is the Director of Spiritual Services and Faith Based Initiative for Hospice Care. People request his presence as their lives come to an end and look forward to his comforting words and help in preparing their families for the inevitable. Pastor Swick's commitment to the community and the people in need is recognized by many. His never ending quest to "Blanket the Homeless", to help with his church's food pantry, to distribute clothing, toys and personal hygiene products to not only his church members but to non-members as well is greatly appreciated. People are not judged, but lifted up by his ministries. This is a man who loves people and let's God direct his efforts and direction. He wears the love of Jesus Christ openly and never fails to share the Good News. He is admired by many, yet his humble attitude is one of his great qualities. I cannot say enough good things about this fine man and his accomplishments.

- Reginald C. Trefethen Jr.
Executive Director
US Programs, Appalachia
World Vision

Over the years I've communicated with Pastor Howard on a personal and professional level many, many times. He has always been kind, thoughtful and insightful. Howard's faith and grace are inspiring.

- Hoppy Kercheval
Host, Metronews Talkline
Vice President Operations
West Virginia Radio Corporation

Pastor Howard Swick is truly a man after God's heart. He walks worthy of his calling as a Pastor and father. I have had the opportunity to work with him at Hospice Care; where he ministers to the needs of our patients and families. In addition to his work as a Chaplain and Director in hospice and Pastor, I have the opportunity to work with him ministering to children and youth. He is an awesome man of God.

- Dale Derby
Vice President Clinical Services
Hospice Care Corporation

If I used one word to describe Howard Swick it would be authentic. It's easy to find characters today but hard to find character – that is until you meet Howard.

- Dale B. Miller
President
West Virginia Radio Corporation

I've known Pastor Howard for several years now. As a friend I've particularly seen these attributes clearly evident in his life: He has a wonderful family! He has a heart after God. Howard and Benita love the people that God has placed under their pastoral care. Pastor Swick is also active in serving his community where he has gained the highest respect among its leaders.

-Dr. James D. Curtis
President
West Virginia Christian University

Howard Swick is a walking illustration of inspiration and motivation for living a good life. I will always remember the day he walked into my hospice program and I thought to myself "there is no way we can fail". His energy and enthusiasm for people and reaching out to families in their time of need is truly inspiring to those who work beside him.

I would recommend this book to anyone who wants to be inspired by someone who lives life to do just that everyday – Howard. Howard uses many sources to reach people of all ages and always with a smile and humor. In this day of dark clouds, I know this book "XV - fifteen" will serve as a fountain of daily motivation to serve.

- Malene Davis
President
Hospice Care Corporation

THE VISION

"WE WILL DO WHATEVER IT TAKES TO REACH THIS FORGOTTEN GENERATION! WE BELIEVE THAT THEY HAVE BEEN CHOSEN FOR THE GREATEST MOVE OF GOD THAT THIS PLANET HAS EVER SEEN! WE BELIEVE THAT TO REACH A <u>RADICAL</u> GENERATION, YOU MUST BE <u>RADICAL</u>!"

Pastors
Howard &
Benita
Swick

TO THE READER

"XV" is a book about fifteen years of life. How God strengthens His children and gives them the wisdom and power to LIVE LIFE in the way that He has planned, not in the way that man has created....

"XV" takes you through fifteen years of stories, personal testimonies, blogs, Bible studies, spiritual thoughts, poems, biblical philosophy, and teachings from Pastor / Chaplain Howard Swick.

It is the story from a young minister's eyes, filled with stories, blogs, poems, thoughts, and messages that will make you smile, make you cry, and will bring you closer to God's destiny for your life through the Glory of His Son Jesus Christ and through the power of His Holy Spirit!

In saying all of that, you may now take the voyage through the past fifteen ("XV") years into the world from a young minister's eyes.

ENJOY!

PREFACE

"The poems, blogs, and stories I share in this book are very dear to my heart. Some of the names and situations had to be changed a bit to protect the privacy of folks. The spiritual content of the many testimonies have not been altered in any form or fashion."

Pastor Howard

DESTINY

I have a Destiny. I have a purpose. I know I have been created by a Creator, and placed here in this place for this time! But as I look through my eyes I see my future, and it looks dark. I leave the place where I'm at to search. I see a way out! I jump at the chance to escape. Suddenly I'm in the hands of a stranger and my Destiny has shifted. I know in my heart that he now controls my Destiny. Something that feels so right could not be wrong for me? So I walk deeper with the stranger, away from the place I was created to dwell, and into a strange realm. I feel confused, lost, empty. The void I try to fill is growing with each step I take. My flesh says "go ahead", but my heart says turn back; my mind is silent. So I walk deeper with the stranger, away from the place I was created to dwell, and into a strange realm.

Now I am afraid, the wind begins to blow, I feel my heart beat, pounding… The wind is blowing stronger and stronger. I feel myself expanding and growing with each gush of air. My innermost being is being stretched. I take on a different look, a new look. A voice on the inside of me wants to be back in the place that I was created and destined to be. But I'm in too deep; I can't turn back. Can I turn back? I walk deeper with the stranger, away from the place that I was created to dwell, and into a strange realm.

*T*he wind still blows; my flesh is cold and stretched. I'm at the point break, when waves crash down on the shore. Then I experience a twist of fate, an unexplained turn of events. I find myself at an interchange. I hear the voice of the stranger pulling me to the left. I want to go, but I feel a voice drawing me to the other side.

Right or Left?

*W*here is my Destiny to be found? To go with the voice of the stranger could mean certain death, but my flesh desires! I hear the voice from the right calling me home. Could this be my Creator? Could I return? Would it ever be the same?

Right or Left?

*M*y Destiny is now laid in my hands...my decision...

*M*y Decision is MY Creator!

"But as for me and my house, we will serve Jehovah." Joshua 24:15

MY JOY MAKER -
"MINI ME"

*A*fter four years of marriage, running a youth ministry, carrying full time jobs (my wife and I both), and taking care of our dog, we decided that it was time to extend our family and have a child. I was so excited when I found out we were pregnant, but it took only a short time for me to realize that "we" weren't pregnant, but it was "SHE" who was pregnant! Over nine months, I watched as my life quickly began to change and my tiny, little loving wife that I had grown to love so dearly, turned into an offspring from the pits of split personality and hyper-emotionalville.

My wife led praise and worship at the church and on Thursday night and Sunday morning everyone who walked near her knew to walk on eggshells. My wife was in a lot of pain and was tired from the pregnancy and working midnight shift at her fulltime job; then the time came for our lives to change.

That spring night we packed her bags, drove to the hospital about thirty minutes away and settled in for the long night. The news of the labor traveled around town and by midnight there was about twenty youth and church family filling the waiting room and the hallway at the hospital. They said when the baby was being born, all of our guests came to the door of the delivery room and started to pray. It must have worked because the actual hard labor time was only fifteen minutes. Over the next few hours, dozens of young people filled the room with prayer and gifts.

I'll never forget that day and the first time I picked up my little baby (who by the way looks just like me) and held her in my arms. I wondered if I had what it takes to be a good dad. Could I do a just job according to God's Word in raising this child? I remember holding her so close and wondering how anyone could ever love anyone else anymore than I loved this baby…then I blinked, and she was no longer a little baby anymore, she was a little girl who I was driving to school. WOW! Where did time go? One day we were feeding her a bottle, and now she's off to school. These days I cherish every little thing that I do with little joy maker, Hannah. She has her mom's intelligence, her dad's wit, and a solid foundation of Jesus even at a young age. I know that she will go far in life.

My Hannah is becoming a musician like her mother. She has started to take piano lessons; she also plays the saxophone, guitar, and many more instruments to come. In school she is a straight "A" student. I know God has a plan for her life, and her mom and I are learning to trust God and the Bible when it says that if you bring up a child according to His Word they will not depart from it! I realize that I'm only a couple of blinks away from giving her away to a husband. (That terrifies me.)

Let me leave the story with this: if you have children, don't take the time that you have with them for granted. Time is a precious gift, and time is so short. Cherish the time you have with your kids while they're young! Our kids are truly our greatest ministry! And whatever you do... Don't Blink!

"Hannah, no matter how old you get, you will always be Daddy's Little Girl..." *I LOVE YOU!*

AN ANGEL NAMED KAITIE

I'll never forget the way that I received the news about my second child. I was in my accountant's office filing our taxes when I had to call my wife to get her social security number. After she gave me her number and some brief dialog, she asked, and I quote... "How much money will we get back this year? I'm pregnant. How's your day?"

My heart stopped for a moment and after leaving the accountant's office I called her on my car phone and said as loving as I could... "WHAT!!!" It was true, and if hindsight is 20/20, then the things I know now I wish I would have known then.

At first I wasn't happy about the new baby. You see, my Hannah (my oldest child) was still only a baby herself and we were just getting the hang of this parent stuff. Now the thought of two babies in the house at the same time... I had just accepted a new job with a radio station and my wife (Benita) had just quit her job and become a full time homemaker/Youth and

Music Minister. It was obvious that my life was about to take a new turn, but I had no idea what we were about to face.

Benita's pregnancy this time was different. She was sick often and she hurt a lot. Early in the pregnancy the doctor found a heart murmur in the baby and we began to pray. I knew that God gave us this child that was inside my wife, and I knew that God would watch over her for us. Some folks told us that abortion might be a better option, but this wasn't just a thing inside of my wife, it was a human being - a life - a baby!!! When the day arrived, after a very long and unsure nine months, my crew of young people from the church, our Pastors, some family members, and my wife and I headed to the hospital and we prayed. The birth this time was even easier than it was with my Hannah. The actual hard labor this time was less than five minutes. The first time I saw my Kaitlin, I fell in love all over again. She was a beautiful four pound miracle but at that time I had no idea what a miracle really was. I was about to find out… she was SO small; I held her in one hand as I loved on her and welcomed her into the world.

At that time Kaitlin's heart seemed to be fine, but the nurse told us that she had a cleft palate (about one in five hundred kids are born with a cleft), so we thanked God for her and we prayed. Then, about five hours later, we found out what it was like to have your world fall completely apart. As I watched my tiny newborn girl try to eat, I suddenly saw her start to gasp for air and turn blue. The world stood still as her little body turned stiff and began to convulse. The next few minutes seemed like an eternity as they rushed her out of the room and began to resuscitate her. Later that morning we were told that a team of specialists was coming to get her and take her to the University Hospital.

That afternoon we checked Benita out of the local hospital and headed to the University at Morgantown, WV. We were so scared, and I remember we prayed all the way to Morgantown.

As we arrived at the hospital, we were so frightened and unsure about everything. One minute we were holding our little babe, and the next minute we were watching her lay in a bed with tubes and wires coming out of her hooked to machines. At that time there was only one thing to do, and that was to pray. That night we found out that Kaitlin also had a condition along with her cleft called "Pierre Robin Sequence" (about one in thirty thousand kids have it). Kaitlin, who then became Kaitie, had to have two surgeries within the next few months. So right before the winter holiday season (after many tears, hours of prayers, and trips to Morgantown) on a Saturday afternoon we got to bring our now five pound Kaitie home for the first time.

Before we left the hospital I asked one of the physicians on duty about how I could get Kaitie to church the next day. She told me "if I thought that I was going to take that little girl out of the house for the next month that I was crazy." She said "NO CHURCH!!!"

So being the civil person that I am, I told her "if it's crazy to bring a living miracle to the house of God then I'm guilty!" I went on to say, "You see it was the prayers of God's people that saved that little girl's life. It's not IF I'm going to take her to church; the question is HOW I'm going to take her to CHURCH!!! The doctor got so angry that she said "You're crazy!!!" and she stormed out of the room. I never talked to her again (maybe she will read my book).

Kaitie had a feeding tube in her tiny stomach, and she now breathed from the tracheotomy tube in her tiny little throat. She had several monitoring machines wired to her and a breathing machine to moisten her tracheotomy tube. The next morning we loaded up all of Kaitie's machines, and of course her little big sister, and headed off to church to show off our new miracle. But at that time we still had no idea what miracle God had in store for our little Kaitie.

Over the next months we learned to care for Kaitie with special care, but she couldn't hold her food down and she wasn't gaining weight. On her first birthday she weighed nine pounds and was starting to crawl. Soon we got the news that the doctor was going to take out her tracheotomy tube. Things looked as if the worst was in the past. However, two weeks after they removed her trach tube, we found out the most shocking news that no parent ever wants to hear. Our Kaitie had a blood disorder called "Diamond Black Fan Anemia" a sister to leukemia (about one in a million kids are born each year with Diamond Black Fan Anemia).

At that time we were told there was a good chance our little Kaitie would not be with us to celebrate her fourth birthday. WOW! That was hard to swallow. I got so mad at God! I remember that I began to pray, "God, how could you let this happen to me? Me, one of your servants. I gave my life to serve You and this is how you repay me!!!!"

Take a note of how many times "Me" came into my prayer…

Too many times when we pray, we make the prayer about us, not HIM! Through my daughter's sickness I learned a valuable lesson of life; **He's God!** That is all we need to know; that **He's God!** The scripture came to mind from Psalm 46:10: **"Be Still and Know that I'm God."**

If we want to see miracles in our lives, that is all we really need to do, be still and know that He is God! I felt God speak to me and say that we all belong to Him and that includes our children.

So we brought Kaitie to our church family, called the body of Christ together and began to pray like never before. We knew that she was God's child and He loaned her to us for this time. A blanket of prayer covered her and we believed that God would take care of her. During the next few months, we received calls from other believers from around the world throughout West Virginia, Ohio, Pennsylvania, Maryland, Virginia, Tennessee, Florida, North Carolina, Canada, England, France… calls and prayers just poured in.

Over the next six months we went on with our lives. We had good days; we had bad days, and then we had *very bad* days. But through it all God was faithful and He gave us peace, hope, and encouragement through His Holy Spirit.

The Phone Call

Then we received the phone call of a lifetime, one that few people in our shoes ever get. Her doctor called us and told us that Kaitie's body was starting to heal itself and was producing blood cells on its own. The doctor said this was unexplainable and nothing they had done caused this. At that time I knew that we had received our miracle, God was faithful to answer our prayers.

Over the next few years, Kaitie had over 13 surgical procedures, but God has gotten us through them. Her blood is disease FREE! What the doctors said would never produce cells is now *normally producing blood cells*. She is in school and doing very well. "The child will live and not die!" That was the promise from my Heavenly Father!

Now everywhere I go, I tell people that God is faithful, that He loves us so much, and that even today "MIRACLES STILL HAPPEN!!!" People always ask me how I know that miracles still occur, and I smile and tell them that every night I tuck my miracle into bed! I end this story with a word of encouragement to anyone who is battling a sickness. Don't give up on your miracle! Keep fighting and keep the faith until the Lord calls you home. When I pass from this world, I want everyone to know that no sickness took me out, but God simply called me home!

Miracles Still Happen!!

"And these signs shall follow them that believe; In my name shall they cast out devils; they shall speak with new tongues; They shall take up serpents; and if they drink any deadly thing, it shall not hurt them; they shall lay hands on the sick, <u>and they shall recover."</u>

Mark 16:17-18

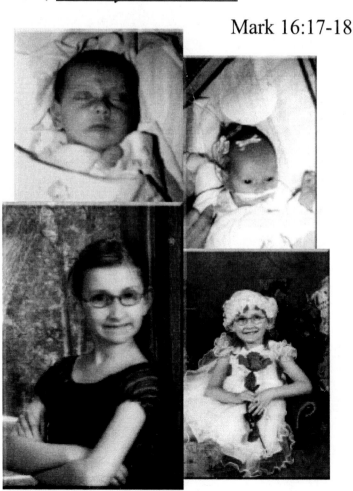

TIME STOOD STILL
& A NATION PRAYED

9/11/2-K-1 started as just another day. Early in the morning the sun arose through the clouds of the night. The Earth was still spinning, and slowly the people who are known as "children of the Giant" began their day. But if hindsight is 20/20, think of the things that we would change in that particular day in history...

Round One: WTC NYC "Building One"

The enemy slyly stepped into the ring like a serpent slivering to its prey. The Giant, totally unaware of the serpent's presence, stood tall in center ring for the whole world to see, holding the championship belt of Freedom, Liberty, and the Pursuit of happiness. The serpent, full of jealousy and hatred, struck first with a blow from behind! It was a hard hit! The Giant was shaken, then the sound of thunder filled the city as smoke and flames filled the sky above.

Who is this enemy from a foreign land and why is his heart full of such hatred and anger? My mind was full of confusion, and then my heart wept, as my spirit cried with vengeance...

First total silence...

Then I heard a sound! A sound of a people of a nation joining together as they watched the whole world halt to a stop... And Time Stood Still And A Nation Prayed!

Round Two: WTC NYC "Building Two"

As wounds appeared on the Giant, the attack continued. The second attack was more violent and more destructive than the first. A cloud of smoke filled the city, and the unbearable heat burned out of control. The Giant seemed to weaken. Could this be the attack that would bring down the Giant and destroy freedom?

My mind was full of confusion, and then my heart wept, as my spirit cried with vengeance...

But once again, I heard a sound! From coast to coast — I heard a sound of a people from a nation — joining together as they watched the whole world halt to a stop... And Time Stood Still And A Nation Prayed!

Round Three: WDC "The Pentagon"

The bell sounded for round three, and the third strike came to the Giant's governmental foundation. The Giant looked tired; he was beginning to look tired and frail. The three strikes seemed to paralyze him. More wounds now appeared on his body, as more fires began to burn. Dark, black smoke now filled another city, and a silent hush came over all...

Then an unexpected shock echoed throughout the world, and seven continents watched in awe as the

Giant of Freedom fell to the ground! Eyes from Asia to Europe, from Africa to Australia, from North America to South America, and from the North Pole to the South Pole – all watched.

Then, from city to city, from coast to coast, from the north, south, east, and west… A nation and a people joined with other tongues and other nations…

And Time Stood Still And A Nation Prayed!

Round Four: Flight 93 "The Final Round"

The fourth strike that came from the enemy was to kick the Giant while he was down, after he had fallen. The enemy went for the kill. His plan was to sever the heart of what we believe, to tear away the structure of peace, and fill our hearts with anger and fear. But suddenly the Giant, as quickly as he had fallen, leaped to his feet!!!

And an army of heroes for liberty took their place in history and fought back! Striking the enemy without consideration for their own lives, they put to sleep the thought that Lady Liberty would ever bow down to terrorism. These heroes stood with patriots from centuries ago, and buried the enemy in his own flames in a field in Pennsylvania!

The Battle's End

After the smoke of the battle cleared away, the sound of a bell of liberty rang throughout the world, and there was still a Lady standing tall and strong in a harbor, holding the torch that lights a nation. A nation under God, standing for freedom and liberty that has become the foundation that it stands upon!

As a nation, let us never take our freedom for granted! And may we never forget that dreadful day when the sleeping Giant was awakened by an enemy of terror. And men and women, dads and moms, brothers and sisters, friends and neighbors, firefighters and office executives, policemen, soldiers and civilians all gave their lives for freedom... and a world watched as Time Stood Still And A Nation Prayed!

Our Nation's Pledge of Allegiance:

I pledge allegiance to the flag of the United States of America, and to the Republic for which it stands: one Nation under God, indivisible, with Liberty and Justice for all.

I'M AN ARMY OF
ONE

I'm a solider, an army of one! If you were asked to look for people to serve or enlist in an army what are some of the qualities you would look for?

- Strength
- Intelligence
- Size
- Talents
- Gifting

God is putting together an army! A Kingdom army… full of His Spirit and equipped with His weapons! The Bible tells us in Romans chapter 8 that we are more than a conqueror. That word *conquer* means, "to gain a decisive victory."

You see, God doesn't look at men as we do. God is looking for two qualities in a people, and He will put together a Spiritual Army <u>that cannot be defeated!</u> God is looking for a passionate people who are passionate about HIM! Passionate for worship, passionate to serve, and passionate to tell others about the goodness and mercy of their God!

Let's look at a man in the Bible who was a army of one. (Read *1 Samuel 17:20 –51.)* Before all of this happened, you see young David the shepherd boy anointed as king in front of his brothers… God wanted a king to be a man after His own heart and David carried those qualities. David knew how to worship and David knew how to serve his father! If you want to become a person after God's heart, then take a lesson from David and learn how to worship and how to serve your Heavenly Father.

David's brother, Eliab, was the oldest and fit the part on the outside to be anointed, but there was something in Eliab that he didn't deal with. Maybe *pride, jealousy, anger, or fear,* but something was different between him and David.

Every one was facing this giant and nobody could defeat him. Note in verse 20 the army was shouting, but when the enemy came to the battlefield they were overcome with fear and fled! It's easy to shout when there is no pressure on you, but where is the shout when your **bank account** isn't just low, but there is nothing in it? When the doctor's report says you have **cancer, heart problems**, or you're about ready to have a **heart attack or a stroke….** Where is the shout when your **son or daughter** is strung out on **drugs** and **sexual perversion,** or when the man or woman that you were planning on being with the rest of your life just **violated your marriage** with another? Where is the shout when your boss comes in with a **pink slip** instead of a raise?

Being an army that is more than a conqueror is having the ability to overcome anything that would come against you! Go ahead and shout during the good times... but God wants to hear someone give a victory shout in the heat of the battle! If you're going through something today, then raise your hands and give a SHOUT of VICTORY even before the battle is over!!!

David's first fight wasn't with Goliath the giant. His first fight to overcome was in the camp of the army of the Lord with his brother Eliab. Sometimes we are looking for the devil outside, in the world, when he is sitting in our church pews. We can never defeat the devil in the bars until we first defeat the devils in our churches.

An Army Of One

I'm a solider; I'm an army of one.
I have been called out; I have been sent on a mission. Now I stand!
I'm standing on the battlefield facing my enemy.
The enemy is tall and strong. Loud shouts of rage come from his mouth.

My mind is afraid, my flesh is weak, but my inner man, my spirit is calling out!
I'm a solider; I'm an army of one! I have been called out! I stand here on a mission. Many have been defeated and many have fallen. I ask myself this question, "Who am I?"
I have no weapons that can stand against his artillery.
If I should pursue this mission I will surely die!
I'm afraid. I do not fear for my life but my fear is that I'll fail my leader.

Who else will fight? Who else will stand? This is my commission! I will fight! My call, my duty!

So I stand! For I'm a solider; I'm an army of one! I have been called out! I stand here on a mission.
One man, one solider, fully armed! Armed and dangerous!
Armed with weapons, but not of this world; the weapons that I choose are weapons of His Spirit!
I stand, protected with full armor. Now I'm armed and facing my enemy.
Who is this enemy that stands before me? Who is he that would dare to curse my Creator, my Lord, my God?

He tries to intimidate me, taunting me as he had done in the past to many others. But I know who I am!
I'm a solider; I'm an army of one! I have been called out! I'm a man on a mission.
Full of power and a vision to see victory! I am the called out one! I'm the one whom my Creator has chosen.

I can win, I must win, and I will win! I am not alone!

I'm an army of one! One man full of the Holy Spirit and backed by an army of ten thousand angels. I'm commissioned and authorized by the one and only true living God. I'm an army of one! Suddenly something changes. Suddenly the enemy doesn't look as big or as powerful as he did before.

I stare into his soul. I see a glimpse of fear.
I look around as I take my position on the battlefield.
I stand, even before the battle begins, in a position of victory.

I have already seen the end results of this war.
I know the final outcome. My confidence overtakes
me….I strike!

Like the sound of thunder and the speed of lightning,
it's a direct hit. For a split second time seems to stand
still. Then like a hundred foot giant red wood falling
to the hand of the lumberjack that struck it.
I watch the giant fall to the ground… His followers
hush as the saints cry victory. Then with the power
of God that fills me I strike again; stripping the life
from his body.

Knowing who I am I stand in victory.
I cannot be defeated!
I am a mighty army! His army!!!
An army of one!
Filled with His Spirit, strengthened by His power,
and armed with His weapons.

I'm an army of one!!!

**What shall we then say to these things?
If God be for us, who can be against us?
Romans 8:31 KJV**

WHO'S YOUR JESUS?

*I*n the Christian world, sometimes it is hard to tell just who is the bigger, Jesus or the devil. We spend so much time praying that the devil will leave us alone that we forget that God has blessed us, is blessing us, and will continue to bless us!

When Jesus allowed Himself to be arrested, beaten, and hung on the cross, He said three words that sealed our destiny… *"It is finished"* (John 19:30). What did He mean when He said those words? What was finished? Or can I ask, who was finished?

I believe that when Jesus said *"It is finished"*, He was making reference to the past, present, and the future (our future). I believe that our salvation was finished on that cross, and there is nothing that we can do to earn it; it's a free gift. But our salvation is more than just a 'get out of hell free' card! It's more than just our ticket to Heaven! In Romans chapter 8, the Bible says **we** are now, because of what Jesus did on the cross, heirs to the throne of God! Think about that for just a minute. What is God saying to the body of the church?

What Jesus has, He has given to us (His children). Everything Jesus has, He has given to us (His children). The only thing that we need to do is to reach out and receive it. Sometimes we spend so much time trying to do things for the Kingdom and trying to earn our Fathers love, grace, and mercy that we get distracted from the New Testament GRACE that the early church was built upon.

God is not angry at you! God loves you so much that He gave you the gift of His only Son. The Son, Jesus, loves you so much that He gave you not only eternal life, but He also gave you His right as a Son of the True and ONLY LIVING GOD! So what does this mean? It means that whatever God's Son, Jesus had/has; now you, being bought on the cross by Jesus' blood, also have! With the power of God's Spirit in us, we have the ability to see and accomplish "greater things" than Jesus did when He walked on the earth (John 1:50).

I believe that the church in America is about ready to be awakened to a revelation of who their God really is, and who they are with the Holy Spirit in and working through them. It's time that we, the church and God's children, stop looking for someone or something to blame for the circumstances that we find ourselves in. Stop giving the devil so much credit! What could happen if the church in America, the most blessed nation on the planet, began to shrink the devil and all of our daily problems and offences and joined together with one voice and praised, and worshiped, and prayed to our God in one accord? The power of the Most High would begin to move through our lives like never before. We would see miracles and healings throughout the land. Our government would turn around and go back to the morality that our forefathers built our nation on. The Bible says that the government shall be upon his shoulders (Isaiah 9:6). Let me end with this; Church, we need to know at all times who our Jesus really is! And who we are in Him!

JOHN 1:1-5

1. In the beginning was the Word, and the Word was with God, and the Word was God.

2. The same was in the beginning with God.

3. All things were made by him; and without him was not any thing made that was made.

4. In him was life; and the life was the light of men.

5. And the light shineth in darkness; and the darkness comprehended it not.

JOHN 1:10-14

10. He was in the world, and the world was made by him, and the world knew him not.

11. He came unto his own, and his own received him not.

12. But as many as received him, to them gave he power to become the sons of God, even to them that believe on his name:

13. Which were born, not of blood, nor of the will of the flesh, nor of the will of man, but of God.

14. And the Word was made flesh, and dwelt among us, (and we beheld his glory, the glory as of the only begotten of the Father,) full of grace and truth.

The Word of
God became a
Living Being
through Jesus!

Who's your
Jesus?

He is the True
Living Word of
God!

FELLOWSHIP

We Who Believe and Receive Jesus Are Part Of The GREAT FAMILY of God!
Eph 1:3-5, 2:19-22

*W*hen we were saved, we became a part of a great family, "the family of God." God is our Father, our Heavenly Daddy! And all who know Him are now our brothers and sisters. Think about this, we are even related to each other by blood, the blood of Jesus! I like to think of my new blood type as "JC Positive!" And now, because of what Jesus did for us, all of God's family now have His blood type.

Just as an earthly father wants his children to love one another, God is also very concerned that His children love and accept one another as well. He desires that we would be united together to do His work!

God has a purpose for His Church. God's purpose is to have His Church, "God's family on earth", to be strong throughout all the earth. Just think about how powerful the Church would become if we all worked together with His agenda and His will in mind not ours.

When Jesus prayed He said "Thy will be done on earth as it is in Heaven." Let this be a lesson to the local church that "Thy will" (God's will) be done, **not my will!!!**

HOW CAN WE FIT IN TO THE BODY OF CHRIST?

Quite often I'm asked this question, "How do we fit into the local church?" That's easy; you can fit in by being an involved part of a local church body. When we all fit in and take our place of service, then the church will grow into God's perfect vessel on earth **(Eph 4:11-16).**

• Start by finding a local church that is preaching the Word of God and is open to the operation of the gifts of the Spirit. Once He (God) has given you a church, become part of it! Identify with it and be very committed and loyal to the people. Remember, these are your family members.

• Then at all times, we need to submit to the authority in God's church. God has given us "Pastors and Elders" folks who feed and protect the people of God **(Heb. 13:17).**

• Start to develop relationships with other people in the church. Find people you feel comfortable with and then pray, counsel, share, and witness with one another. Life goes a little better when you're not walking alone! Love everyone, even those people who rub on you the wrong way… Make an effort to befriend all of the people at church and if a problem arises between you and a brother or sister, then solve it immediately!

Talents are given and gifts are cultivated, so be open to filling areas of needs in the church with your talents and gifts that God gave you. This is how you build the church into the Power Church that God has planned for us **(Rom. 12:6-8).**

Last when the preacher speaks, listen to the message preached and apply it to your life.

WHAT WAS THE POWER
OF THE EARLY CHURCH?

The New Testament Church had four keys:
· *Breaking of bread before God*
· *Teaching the Gospel*
· *Praying with and for one another*
· *Fellowshipping one with another*

Let's start to practice the values that the New Testament Church was built on and watch God's Holy Spirit move in a mighty way.

WALKIN' ON YOUR OWN TWO LEGS!

Walking into our Promised Land:

*B*etween where we are now and where God wants us to be, there is usually a challenge. That challenge is finding the strength within to walk on our own two legs, even when we don't have the strength to do so. With the Israelites, they were in the desert and God wanted them to enter the Promised Land. But in the way of their destiny were giant cities, cities with walls that seemed to extend to the heavens and giants in the land.

In our own personal lives, like the Israelites, the place we are today and the place God wants us to be is usually blocked by a challenge, WALLS or GIANTS! Today, I want to look at the real challenge that Joshua had as he led God's people across the Jordan into the Promised Land.

Moses can only go so far:

Moses could only take the people so far. He led them out of the bondage of Egypt, but God needed a Joshua (a new cutting edge generation, a new way, a new word) to lead the people into the place of the Promised Land - their Destiny...

Joshua 1:1-11

1. Now it came to pass after the death of Moses the servant of Jehovah, that Jehovah spoke to Joshua the son of Nun, and Moses' minister, saying,

2. Moses my servant is dead; now therefore arise, go over this Jordan, and lead all these people, unto the land, which I do give to them, even to the children of Israel.

3. Every place that the sole of your foot shall tread upon, to you have I given it, as I spoke unto Moses.

4. From the wilderness, and this Lebanon, even unto the great river, the river Euphrates, all the land of the Hittites, and unto the great sea toward the going down of the sun (the sun set), shall be your border.

5. There shall not any man be able to stand before thee all the days of thy life. As I was with Moses, so I will be with thee; I will not fail thee, nor forsake thee.

6. Be strong and of good courage; for thou shall cause this people to inherit the land which I swore unto their fathers to give them.

7. Only be strong and very courageous, to observe to do according to all the law, which Moses my servant commanded thee: turn not from it to the right hand or to the left, that thou may have good success wherever thou goes.

8. This book of the law shall not depart out of thy mouth, but thou shall meditate there day and night, that thou may observe to do according to all that is written therein: for then thou shall make thy way prosperous, and then thou shall have good success.

9. Have not I commanded thee? Be strong and of good courage; be not afraid, neither be thou dismayed: for Jehovah thy God is with thee wherever thou goes.

10. Then Joshua commanded the officers of the people, saying,
11. Pass through the midst of the camp, and command the people, saying, Prepare you food; for within three days you are to pass over this Jordan, to go in to possess the land, which Jehovah your God given you to possess it.

Walking With God Through Challenges

Joshua faced the challenge between where he was and where God wanted him. Today we face that same challenge, where we are today and where God wants us! God waited for Moses to die before challenging Joshua to cross the Jordan. When Moses died (I am sure that) Joshua felt alone, and yet God was asking him to face the greatest challenge of his life. I am sure that he felt he was facing this challenge alone. You may be facing a challenge in your life today; don't be surprised if you feel alone. You feel like no one understands. No one knows what you are going through. No matter how lonely you feel in facing your challenges, you must believe that God is with you and will STAY with you through the end. God said He would be with you and never leave you nor forsake you. God was telling Joshua that no matter how big the challenge, or how small the challenge, He's there to see you through it. If you are having family problems, God is there with you. If you are having financial problems, God is there with you. If you are having physical problems, God is there with you. You may feel alone, but trust me when I say God is there with you.

There will be times in your life that the only thing that you can hang on to is that God is with you through each and every circumstance in your life. Whenever

I come up against a challenge I need to know God has been working on that challenge even before I get there. God has given us every place where we set our feet as He promised to Moses. When Joshua came up to his challenge, God had already been working on it. The thing that will get us from where we are today, to where God wants us to be, is how we view the challenges that are before us. The ten spies saw the challenge as too great. Caleb and Joshua saw how great God is. **What God is telling me is put the challenge in the proper perspective. Look at how big your GOD really is then look at the challenge before you.**

If I find myself terrified or discouraged by a situation, did I not prepare for that situation? Did I not trust God in the challenge? The Bible teaches us not to be terrified; and not to be discouraged, for the Lord your God will be with you wherever you go. The people had not forgotten the failed challenge of their parents 40 years ago. They were not going to murmur or hesitate in entering the Promised Land. Not one word of grumbling is found.

CHURCH:

IT'S TIME THAT WE STOP LOOKING AT THE PAST AND BEGAN TO WALK INTO THE PROMISED LAND THAT GOD HAD PROMISED OUR FATHERS... WALKING ON OUR OWN TWO LEGS!

THE TRIBE &
THE STICKS!!!

*W*e took some of our youth to a conference and one of the guest speakers was a missionary from "the land down under." He preached about one of the tribes from another country that he had ministered to. This tribe would have radical worship services every night and pray to their gods. As they worshiped they would bang sticks on the ground to make a drum beat. The sticks were carved with demonic symbols of their gods and had stones and jewels attached to them.

After many visits from this missionary they received the message of Jesus and became Christians. After the tribe became Christians they continued to have nightly worship services, but instead of worshiping other false gods, they were now worshiping the True Living God! As they worshiped the false gods by banging the sticks, they now had "Christ Sticks" that they would bang to the ground making music as they sang songs to Jehovah God. The chief of the tribe gave the missionary a Christ Stick or a staff that he had previously used to worship Jehovah God. The stick had a dove carved into it representing God's Holy Spirit, and a cross carved into it as a symbol of Christ dying on a cross for our sins. It also had several hash marks carved into a side representing each person that the chief had won to Jesus.

As the missionary preached to the young folks, they became inspired to make their own "Christ Sticks." I think you most likely know where I'm going with this story. Our kids from the church youth group caught word of the "Christ Sticks" and started to make their own sticks. Some carved Bible verses in their sticks, others carved symbols of their faith such as a Christian fish, crosses, the dove, the Ten-Commandment tablets...well, you get the picture. During youth worship night the teens would show up with their "Christ Sticks" and worship God with "all of their might." I felt the sticks were harmless and a neat way that the younger generation could make a banner or statement for their faith! I saw the sticks equal to an adult bringing a tambourine into church and banging it while they worshiped their God. Well, all did not agree with me.

The word spread about my wife and I as Youth Pastors allowing the kids to bring sticks into God's house. The so called "Christian community" in our region lashed out against us in a mighty way. The church elders and Senior Pastor began to receive phone calls about the sticks. One local Pastor (who is still a Pastor in my county) told my Pastor at the time to remove us as his Youth Pastors due to the sticks. The youth ministry began to see hundreds of kids coming into the church and getting saved, delivered from drugs, alcohol, perversion, you name it, and the local Christian community focused on the sticks!

The "Christ Sticks" lasted for a couple of years, but 12 years later I still hear the religious community talking about those sticks. I estimate that over the two year period during the "Christ Sticks", we saw over 1000 teenagers come into the Kingdom and receive Jesus into their hearts. And during that time, not one local Pastor ever came to my wife or me and said one positive word about what God was doing in our community. I guess they were all consumed with the Sticks.

I can still see hundreds of teens packed into an old skating rink converted into a church, worshiping their God with thirty or forty "Christ Sticks." They became a Tribe for Jesus, and they really didn't care what their peers thought, nor did they care what the religious folks thought. They would worship and dance before God for hours at a time. We didn't have to cheerlead or prime the kids, it was God's Holy Spirit that led them to these great services and it was God's Holy Spirit that controlled each service! As they worshiped God with their sticks, I saw a glimpse of the Tribe of Judah manifesting before me.

We spend so much of our time during worship services battling pride! It's pride that tells us that we can't allow those kids to bring a stick into God's House, it's pride that tells us not to raise our hands to God or not to dance before His throne. The close minded arrogance and pride that the so-called Christians showed during those couple of years still concerns me today. If a young person wants to worship God, LET THEM! If they want to dance before God, clap their hands, raise their hands, bang a tambourine or bang a stick… LET THEM!!! Trust me, there are worse things that a teenager could be doing today other than banging a stick while they worship God!

Now for those religious folks that say, "Sticks aren't in the Bible." Well I could go on from Genesis to Revelation about how folks used sticks to worship God. How many times did Moses and Aaron use a stick to show God's power and bring Glory to God? And in the great book of Revelation, we're told that Christ Jesus Himself holds in His hand, a scepter, which is a type of STICK! I wonder if when Christ comes back for His Bride if those same critics that condemned those kids and their "Christ Sticks" will condemn Him for caring His Scepter Stick. Just a thought…

Let me end this story with a challenge to Christians. Let's join together and seek ways to reach this next generation for God's Kingdom. We will do whatever it takes to reach this next generation and see them saved! Amen?

**Make a joyful noise unto the LORD, all ye lands.
Psalm 100:1 KJV**

GIVING IT UP TO
A STRANGER

She was only fifteen when she came to our youth group. We had a youth lock-in and one of our youth invited her to attend. When my wife and I first met her, we knew that she had something special. She had been raised her whole life in church, coming from a very religious family. The church that she came from was a very traditional church. She was looking for something else, something exciting, and something real. Our aggressive, cutting edge style of youth ministry seemed to be the answer that she was searching for.

Quickly she became a part of our youth ministry, and over the next three years we saw God move in her life in such a radical way! She was very popular at high school, so when she became "Sold Out" to Jesus, it got the attention of the whole school. Several young people came into our youth ministry through her testimony.

After a short time in our group she began to date a young man in our group. Even in that she was still faithful to her commitment to God and remained pure. They met with my wife and I many times and shared their temptations to experiment with their sexual desires. We shared God's Word with them and explained God's desire for their lives, that He had a perfect destiny for their lives! And His Will was for both of them to remain pure until their wedding night.

She dated this young man for about a year and then she dated a few other boys off and on over the next few years, but all and all she stayed pure to her commitment to God. It was her senior year in school and she had just turned eighteen when she got a part time job at a local restaurant. One night she had gotten into a fight with her father before leaving for work. She was so upset, and she had said that she wanted to call my wife and I but she decided not to. She went ahead and worked her waitress shift. By the end of her shift she was ready to go home when he came into the restaurant where she worked. He was a twenty-five year old man who had been married and divorced twice.

Later on we found out that she really had no strong love relationship with her father. This night we saw how Satan used this lack of relationship with her dad to bring this pure young lady down. After talking to this twenty-five year old stranger, she made to biggest mistake of her whole life, a decision that she would soon regret and a decision that she could never take back.

She left that restaurant with this stranger and went with him down a dark road. He stopped by a local station, bought her alcohol and pulled the car over. After she drank several beers, he began to kiss and make over her. She had saved herself for her wedding night for eighteen years, and out of nowhere she freely gave herself, and all of her innocence, to a stranger. She said that she had not intended to go "all the way" with him; she just wanted to "play around." But before she knew it they were having intercourse and she said that she just laid there and cried hoping it would end soon. She may have been intoxicated, but she still knew that she had broken a commitment before God. She had a weak moment and placed herself into a position where she simply gave away a gift that she had saved for her future husband.

The young lady was restored back to God later on, but the consequence for her sinful actions was the loss of her innocence that she will never get back. In our so called "if it feels good then do it society" that we live in today, the message that young people are receiving is "go ahead and do what you want; it's your body, your life, and your choice." Just remember this, all sin has consequences, and the Bible teaches us that the wage of sin is death. But the good news is that no matter haw bad you've been, no matter what you've done, God's grace and mercy can and will cover you. Isn't our God a Good God?

Let me end this story with a message to parents. You (not a school system, not a Sunday school teacher, not a preacher) have a responsibility to teach your kids about sex and what the Bible says about being pure and clean. God designed sex as a bonding between a man and his wife! I believe that about 10% of sex is physical and 90% emotional and spiritual. On TV and movies our kids learn that it's ok to sleep around with anyone and everyone. We as Christians need to teach our kids God's truth about sex, love, and marriage. The world begins to teach our kids their views on sex at a very early age, so don't wait to discuss this Biblical truth with your sons and daughters. Teach them and continue to reinforce God's Word with them daily! Then keep the communication lines open at all times! Let your kids know that talking to mom or dad is a safe place. Sometimes we need to stop talking and begin to listen to our young people more. Also, before your kids become teenagers, develop a plan for dating. And no matter what, stick to the plan! Don't compromise! I encourage fathers to take their sons and daughters out and have "the talk" with them and give them a token of their purity. These Purity rings (also called chastity rings or promise rings) are a token of a vow made before God and imply that the wearer will remain abstinent until it is replaced with a wedding ring.

And now here is a message for the young people. The best wedding gift you can give to your spouse on your wedding night is the gift of your virginity and purity. I challenge every young person to make a vow before God to your future spouse that regardless of what you have done in the past, but starting now you will remain pure until your wedding night. Then join with your Christian peers and your Pastor or Youth Pastor and stay accountable to your commitment.

But now being made free from sin, and become servants to God, ye have your fruit unto holiness, and the end everlasting life. For the wages of sin is death; but the gift of God is eternal life through Jesus Christ our Lord.   Romans 6:22-23

SOAK IN GOD'S RIVER

Baptism of The Holy Spirit: Full immersion in the Spirit of God.

*I*n the Old Testament, the Prophet Joel prophesied that God would **"pour out His Spirit upon <u>all flesh</u> in the last days" (Joel 2:28-29).**

This promise is fulfilled in our receiving the Baptism of the Holy Spirit **(Acts 2:14-21).** Now the FULL power of God is given to us through God's Spirit! Prior to ascending into Heaven, after His bodily resurrection, Jesus promised to send the Holy Spirit to the members of His church **(John 14:16-18).** Now Jesus can continue His earthly ministry in and through us by the authority and power of the Holy Spirit.

Being filled with God's Holy Spirit isn't something that Pentecostals made up. God commands us to be filled with His Spirit after we repent and are saved **(Acts 2:38-39).** This is a total immersion into the Holy Spirit and a release of His power in and through us **(John 7:38-39).**

READ: Revelation 22:1-5 KJV

¹And he shewed me a pure river of water of life, clear as crystal, proceeding out of the throne of God and of the Lamb. ²In the midst of the street of it, and on either side of the river, was there the tree of life, which bare twelve manner of fruits, and yielded her fruit every month: and the leaves of the tree were for the healing of the nations. ³And there shall be no more curse: but the throne of God and of the Lamb shall be in it; and his servants shall serve him: ⁴And they shall see his face; and his name shall be in their foreheads. ⁵And there shall be no night there; and they need no candle, neither light of the sun; for the Lord God giveth them light: and they shall reign for ever and ever.

The word RIVER is: *potamos* (Pronounced pot-am-os') and is defined as a current, brook (as drinkable), running water, movement, a flood, a stream, water, to be accepted. The River of God is a place of movement. Too many people go to church every week, but their Spirit isn't moved and God's Holy Spirit isn't moving in them! God's Spirit flows like a current. When a river flows, it doesn't need man's help… the same is true with God's Spirit. When the anointing is flowing, it doesn't need our help (most of the time we just get in the way). I like the last definition "to be accepted" the church should be a place where people feel welcome and accepted. If sinners are not welcomed in your church, then I think it's time that the church leaders take a long hard look at the Bible and Jesus' ministry.

Now Read: Ezekiel 47:1-12

¹Afterward he brought me again unto the door of the house; and, behold, waters issued out from under the threshold of the house eastward: for the forefront of the house stood toward the east, and the waters came down from under from the right side of the house, at the south side of the altar.

²Then brought he me out of the way of the gate northward, and led me about the way without unto the utter gate by the way that looketh eastward; and, behold, there ran out waters on the right side.

³And when the man that had the line in his hand went forth eastward, he measured a thousand cubits, and he brought me through the waters; the waters were to the ankles.

⁴Again he measured a thousand, and brought me through the waters; the waters were to the knees. Again he measured a thousand, and brought me through; the waters were to the loins.

⁵Afterward he measured a thousand; and it was a river that I could not pass over: for the waters were risen, waters to swim in, a river that could not be passed over.

⁶And he said unto me, Son of man, hast thou seen this? Then he brought me, and caused me to return to the brink of the river.

⁷Now when I had returned, behold, at the bank of the river were very many trees on the one side and on the other.

⁸Then said he unto me, These waters issue out toward the east country, and go down into the desert, and go into the sea: which being brought forth into the sea, the waters shall be healed.

⁹And it shall come to pass, that every thing that liveth, which moveth, whithersoever the rivers shall come, shall live: and there shall be a very great multitude of fish, because these waters shall come thither: for they shall be healed; and every thing shall live whither the river cometh.

[10]And it shall come to pass, that the fishers shall stand upon it from Engedi even unto Eneglaim; they shall be a place to spread forth nets; their fish shall be according to their kinds, as the fish of the great sea, exceeding many.

[11]But the miry places thereof and the marishes thereof shall not be healed; they shall be given to salt.

[12]And by the river upon the bank thereof, on this side and on that side, shall grow all trees for meat, whose leaf shall not fade, neither shall the fruit thereof be consumed: it shall bring forth new fruit according to his months, because their waters they issued out of the sanctuary: and the fruit thereof shall be for meat, and the leaf thereof for medicine.

We say in our spiritual lives that we will step into the water or the anointing of the Holy Spirit, but just up to my ankles. Then some say, I'll step up to my knees, then there are others that say, I'll go in up to my waist. You see the problem is that in each case we are still in control! That's our nature, being in control. But you can see the problem. God demands for us to yield our control to Him, but our flesh wants to be in control. So we always have a tug of war over control between flesh and spirit. I believe that if you want true freedom in your life, then you must first give God **total control** of everything in your life. Everything means everything, your job, family, hobbies, finances… Everything!

At the end of our text in Ezekiel, the angel called Ezekiel out into the river so far that the river had complete control of him. Think about it, this is the position that God needs us to be in, if we want to achieve God's Full Destiny for our lives! We must allow God to have Total Control of our lives! Remember, Jesus is either the Lord of your all or not Lord at all.

MISSION 3:16

*A*re you sick and tired of being sick and tired? Are you longing for a better life, a better way?

Are bill collectors clogging up your phone line and tearing down your front door?

Are you lonely and looking for love in what seems to be all of the wrong places?

Are you worn down from taking 15 different types of feel good pills?

Is your marriage on the rocks and about to become a divorce statistic?

Are you worried about your children's future and the direction in life that they are taking?

Are your enemies getting the best of you, and are you tired of being angry at the world all of the time?

If you answered yes to one or more of the previous questions then stop what you're doing and write this number down... 3-16, that's 3-16...

It's in these numbers that you'll find the miracle formula that you've been searching for...

It's this easy; just open up your Bible, translation of your choice, to the Gospel of John chapter 3, verse 16...

Read about how God loved every person in the world so much that He gave us His only Son, and how all you have to do is receive Him and you'll live throughout eternity!

No, it's not a pill. It's more than just a formula; it's a way of life - a better life!!!

God's phone lines are open. Call today, call now...

Mission 3-16... it's your way into a better, healthier, wealthier, stress free, prosperous, blessed, and happier life!!!

To learn more about Mission 3-16 and other great scriptures that can change your life, read your Bible and get to know your God on a personal level .

This is good stuff; it'll change your life!!!

MISSION 3-16...

For God so loved the world, that he gave his only begotten Son, that whosoever believeth in him should not perish, but have everlasting life.
John 3:16

PRAYER

Spending Quality Time With God

*T*he best way to get to know someone is to converse with that person often. Talk to them. God longs for you to know Him; He wants His people to talk to Him. The Bible is full of invitations to enter into a deep personal relationship with God the Father.

"If you seek Him, He will let you find Him." (I Chron. 28:9)

Speaking of those who would soon become followers of Jesus Christ, God says,

"I will give them a heart to know me, for I am the Lord" (Jeremiah 24:7).

Prayer is a conversation with God. It includes speaking to God and hearing from God. Remember a conversation goes both ways. Sometimes you talk, and sometimes you listen.

Time To Pray And Have Fellowship With God

I teach that a part of prayer time is reading your Bible. You eat food daily to stay alive, right? God's Word is your spiritual food that our inner man needs to eat for survival. The next step is Praise Time! Praise Him at all times, in all things! Read Psalms 100:4. Praise and worship is the door to the courts of God the Most High (the door to the Holy of Holies).

Psalm 100 KJV

¹Make a joyful noise unto the LORD, all ye lands.

²Serve the LORD with gladness: come before his presence with singing.

³Know ye that the LORD he is God: it is he that hath made us, and not we ourselves; we are his people, and the sheep of his pasture.

⁴Enter into his gates with thanksgiving, and into his courts with praise: be thankful unto him, and bless his name.

⁵For the LORD is good; his mercy is everlasting; and his truth endureth to all generations.

There is an unseen power in praise and worship! Praise and worship is what we were created to do, and we who believe in Him will spend eternity giving Him praise!

After praise and worship, begin to thank Him for all that He's done in your life. (Read First Thessalonians 5:18 and Psalms 95:2.) Thanksgiving needs to be our lifestyle as a born again believer. Give thanks to God because He is God in any and all circumstances. When we enter into the presence of God - thanksgiving is a natural response. Learn to give thanksgiving now and when we get to Heaven we will be giving thanks throughout eternity.

Now the biggie... "Confession Time". Read First John 1:9.

If we confess our sins, he is faithful and just to forgive us our sins, and to cleanse us from all unrighteousness (1 John 1:9).

Confess what is on the inside to God. Trust me, you won't shock Him! He already knows what's on the inside, and He commands us to confess it with our mouth (words are a powerful thing).

After the confession, now you can petition Him.

Ask, and it shall be given you; seek, and ye shall find; knock, and it shall be opened unto you (Matthew 7:7).

Don't be afraid to ask God for what you need. You can ask Him for His help, and the Bible says He will freely give it. God says He will supply ALL your needs (I John 5:14-15).

All of your needs are not just physical! Sometimes you need peace, joy, love, strength, etc… **God loves His Children and He wants to BLESS THEM!**

Now we come to the toughest part, listening!

This is the hardest part of fellowship with God. Sometimes we need to be still after all is said and done and listen to what God is saying. Our own words and preconceived thoughts can be our worst enemy!!! A conversation works two ways and more than likely God will not speak to you in an audible voice, but He will impress certain things on your heart. When God speaks, you will know it's Him. Sometimes the most important thing we can do is stop talking and listen! There is a reason God gave us two ears and one mouth! He wants us to listen twice as much as we talk. God also speaks through His Word, the Bible. Someone once said, "When I pray, I read my Bible, get on my knees and don't say another word. I just listen to the voice of God."

I believe that we first have to realize we need God. We need God's input in our lives daily and He wants to give it to us. You can pray all the time; you can talk to God anywhere. He's always present and He is always listening to you. Fellowship with God and getting direction from God needs to be our lifestyle if we are a true Christian. God loves you. He cares about what's going on in you life, and He will always listen to you. Remember, if it is important to you, then it is important to God! Start your new committed life by making a vow to God. Vow to God that you, as a believer, will spend time each week in undisturbed fellowship and prayer directly with Him.

Don't make excuses; don't be distracted. Discipline yourself and make NO exceptions! Build an expectation in your mind, and know that God will bless you and that your life can and will get better through a deeper relationship with God! Expect God to do what He says He will do. He will supply your needs in 1 John, and give you the desires of your heart in Psalms. He will give you power to do all things in Philippians, and empower you to do greater things than Jesus himself in Mark. Expect God to talk to you; expect God to answer your prayers.

Expect God to bless you with all of His Glory! After all, you are a child of the Most High.

Now, let's begin to set some goals for our spiritual life. How is my prayer life? Do I pray daily? Do I pray with and for others? Do I pray in faith knowing that God will answer? If we want to see God move in our lives, then we need to get on our knees and pray! Many years ago I listened to a rap song by MC Hammer called *Pray*. It said, "That's why we pray!" This should be the theme song for the church when times get hard – we should say, "That's why we pray!"

SHINE

I awake each morning, and look into Your eyes...

I see your light shining down; Your rays spark and light the sky.

Then You shine!

As I prepare myself for a long day of work, sweat, and toil...

It's unto my world that You turn, and unto my world I know Your love is loyal.

You look down on me, and it's down on me You smile so bright...

It's for You that I left the fears of darkness and entered Your shining light.

It wasn't long ago, that I fell into a sleep of dark dreams...

But I see You bursting through my sky, my life has changed from the seams.

I gleam at You each day, and I know You're with me through the night...

First, You burst through the clouds, then rays of colors fill my sight...

Then You shine!

You shine when I'm in the morning, You light my paths when I cannot see.

You give me water when I thirst, and quench my thirst - You set me free!

And now it's for You that I live, and it's for You that I would die.

For it is the convictions from my heart, that cannot be denied.

Their was a time and place in my life, when in You, I did not believe,

But through Your unchanging love and mercy - it's that I now give and receive.

In the days to come and in the days ahead I now know there is nothing that I cannot do.

For a team that is more than a conqueror and cannot fail is a team of me plus You!

So when I awake in the morning, and I look into Your eyes...

I now know I'll see Your light shining down, and Your rays will spark and light my sky.

And then WE WILL SHINE!!!

Let your light so shine before men, that they may see your good works, and glorify your Father which is in heaven.
Matthew 5:16

XV

YOUTH ATTACK -
IT'S TIME TO FIGHT BACK!

*I*n a Christian nation (regardless of what a select few may say, history shows that the U.S.A. **WAS** founded as a **CHRISTIAN NATION),** Godly values and morality is unseen. A humanistic philosophy has infected our society and it seems that a silent majority has taken a back seat to a minority of unbelievers. This minority group has succeeded in taking God out of the public eye, out of schools and colleges, and out of main stream America. Christianity has become a joke to the Washington and Hollywood elite. As a result, every moral and ethical area of our nation has been declining decade after decade. And the church has set back and done nothing! In this nation, about 80% confess to be Christians. About 75% want public schools to display the Ten Commandments, and about 80% want students to say prayers at graduation ceremonies as part of the official program. About 70% want the Bible used in literature, history, and social studies classes, about 70% want daily prayer to be spoken in the classroom, and about 70% want

77

Creationism taught in public schools… WOW, this is something you'll never hear on CNN.

I feel that our nation has been under attack for decades by the enemy (the devil), and I say, **"It's time to take it BACK!"** I make a public **Declaration of War** on Satan and all of his demons. On a Sunday morning at Haven of Hope Worship Center, my local church, several kids took the first step and became Spiritual Knights in the Lord's Army – Agreeing to fight for their generation. This next generation is too important; we must not allow them to slip away from God's destiny for their lives! Join them and me in this worthy fight to save the next generation, "A Generation Worth Fighting For!!!"

>>> Youth Attack -- It's Time to Fight Back!!! <<<

Youth Attack Poem

IN THE BEGINNING THERE WAS GOD!!!

*G*od so loved the world that he gave His only son, Jesus Christ, so that whoever would believe in Him would never die but have eternal life…

Suppose a man had 100 sheep and one of them strays? Won't he leave the 99 sheep in the hills to look for the one that has strayed? I can guarantee this is the truth: if he finds it, he is happier about it than about the 99 that have not strayed. In the same way, your Father in heaven does not want one of these little ones to be lost.

We have found ourselves living in a corrupt world where wrong is right, and right is a thing of the past.

Our world is a place where an entire generation is unable to recognize the true gift of salvation and suffers daily from abandonment and confusion.

A generation is crying out for help; we must stand together and answer this call!

Here's a girl, shes only 16 years old, teen mistfit she's been called. Totally confused, mentally abused, very unsure about the don'ts and do's. The world around her suddenly fell, as a sinner, she is stricken, headed straight for hell. She's heard God's Word, but refused to believe about this unseen faith that she could receive. If she could have only seen it coming from the start, the spiritual warfare of her heart. Heart, mind, and soul - but now temptations of the world have taken control. She left her home to be with her friends, who now have left her on the streets to die / is it the end?

Broke / hungry, nowhere to turn, just a lost little lamb..."Will this lamb ever learn?"

A happy ending to this story is unseen, she's about to take her life — shes only 16...

Teen suicide in America is on the rise, violence, drugs, and sexual immorality have become a normal everyday occurrence in the war zones that we call the public school system.

On the other side of town there lived a boy, he's also 16 years old, with a mind full of evil and a heart way too cold. He always stood stern, ready for a burn,

79

we'll call him a prodigal son, will he ever return? Day after a day he would run around with thugs, always strapped with a gat' and holding a pipe full of drugs. He was a hanging out with his friends after school one night, when a group of guys got in his face; it was easy to see that they where looking for a fight. So he pulled out his nine m and then he put them to the ground, the wrong time & wrong place is the only defense he found.

A few weeks later he pleaded guilty in court, sentenced to life in prison — a fallen mission — too late to abort. Here's a story of a young boy who took a very wrong turn, just another lost little lamb... "Will this lamb ever learn?"

They say that love will always be a solution to mend, but now life at only 16; could this be his end...

Homosexualty, immorality, sex, abortion on demand, drug abuse, violence, rapes, suicide - the list goes on and on and on…

Christians, can't you see, the youth are dying - they need to be set free! Free from the pain the devil has had planned, for the foundation of the church lies in their hands. We need to band together to heal and suture, for the children of today are the church's future...

SOMEBODY PRAY FOR THEM!!!

Let no man despise thy youth; but be thou an example of the believers, in word, in conversation, in charity, in spirit, in faith, in purity.
1 Timothy 4:12

SIN

Where Did It Start?

Sin is a violation of the law and an offence against God, His Word, and His character. Sin is a pathway to darkness, and a road away from light. When we sin, we carry guilt! Someone once said that "the moral character of a man's actions is determined by the moral state of his heart."

The origin of sin is not a mystery; it started when the devil was thrown out of Heaven as a result of pride! Through the devil and as a result of the fall of man (Adam), sin has entered this world. God permits sin to exist in this imperfect world, but His permitting it in no way makes God the author of sin. Notice that sin began as a result of pride. I believe that all sin falls under pride. Pride is married to rebellion, and every sin is attached to pride and rebellion. Adam's sin (Gen. 3:1-6) consisted in him falling into temptation and eating the forbidden fruit. It involved the sin of pride; Adam wanted to become God-like which is prideful. By sinning Adam became a fugitive from God. He rebelled against his Creator, resulting in losing God's blessing and communion. Through sin Adam's nature became sinful and corrupt.

Now because of the fall of man we are all born into a sinful nature. This is called "original sin." God appointed Adam as the first or head of the human creation, and when he fell, all of human creation fell with him. His affliction became our affliction, and his fall became our fall. But as Adam was the beginning of human sin, Jesus came to earth to become the end of our sin. Since Adam's sin became our sin; Jesus' victory over sin now becomes our victory over sin!

How Much Sin Can I Get By With?

Many times people ask me these questions. "Can I still do this and get to Heaven?" "Can I still sin this much and still make it?" I tell them that they need to refocus their lives. If the only reason you became a Christian is to get to Heaven, then friend you have a very narrow view on Jesus! If you truly know Jesus and have totally committed your whole life to Him, then sin is going to be the last thing on your mind! As Christians, we should be so overwhelmed with God's mercy, goodness, love, forgiveness and grace that we don't want to sin. We know that we all sin, according to the book of Romans, but we should try to abstain from sin daily, even the thought of sin. Today we have too many Christians going around playing games with God and playing with sin… that is a dangerous game! I once read a phrase stating, "Play today and die tomorrow."

I remember reading the story of the Titanic, "the ship that couldn't sink." Hours before the ship went down, right after it hit the iceberg, I read that several large pieces of ice fell on the deck of the ship. The people trusted this man made object so much that they weren't afraid. Instead of evacuating the ship, the people went on as if nothing happened. Some of the young people on board even began to play kick ball with the chunks of ice. Hours later the same ice that they were playing with would soon become their death.

Here in our culture, we have generations of young people playing with sin. As this is happening, the church is standing around doing nothing. Sound familiar? This is a warning to the people that think that sin won't hurt them; the same sin that you're playing with now will soon be your spiritual death.

But now being made free from sin, and become servants to God, ye have your fruit unto holiness, and the end everlasting life. For the wages of sin is death; but the gift of God is eternal life through Jesus Christ our Lord. **Romans 6:22-23**

Because of Adam's sin, the whole world is now in a state of sin, condemnation, moral corruption, guilt, and unrighteousness. Because of sin we are now born spiritually dead!

But I bring you good news; while we were still sinners Christ died for us! Jesus went to the grave taking on the sin of the world, your sin and my sin. Now we who are born into sin and spiritual death can gain life by receiving the gift of salvation that Jesus offers to each of us. Through Jesus we are now born again -

into life. At church we sing the old hymn "Just As I Am". Think about those words.... I can come to God through the Son (Jesus) just as I am. I don't have to clean my life up; when I come to God just as I am, He cleans my life up. He takes away things that are unclean and gives me gifts and blessings that my mind can't comprehend.

Remember, we are all sinners – equally bad and saved by God's grace – equally saved! Now through Jesus my sin is cast away! Through grace, when God sees me He no longer sees my sin, but He now sees Jesus covering me!

Remember this -- "God's Grace is always Greater than sin!!!"

7 Ways To Praise & Worship

*W*e believe that all of the promises that Christianity embrace comes from the covenant God made with Abraham. We as Christians can enjoy over five thousand years of blessings and promises. This is our Inheritance from God through Jesus! Every year at my local church we host a Christian-Hebrew Shabach Service to celebrate our Jewish Inheritance. Everything that we do in the Christian Church is grounded in our Jewish heritage. Below is a list of the seven styles of worship that we do in the modern church that we get from our Jewish heritage.

#1. Lift Holy Hands (YADAH) [YA DA]•

Psalms 18
32. The God that girdeth me with strength, And maketh my way perfect? 33. He maketh my feet like hinds' feet: And setteth me upon my high places. 34. He teacheth my hands to war; So that mine arms do bend a bow of brass.

Psalms 141

1. Jehovah, I have called upon thee; Make haste unto me: Give ear unto my voice, when I call unto thee. 2. Let my prayer be set forth as incense before thee; The lifting up of my hands as the evening sacrifice.

#2. Sacrifice of Praise (*TOWDAH*) *[TOE DA]*

Psalms 50:14

14. Offer unto God the sacrifice of thanksgiving; And pay thy vows unto the Most High:

Psalms 116:17

17. I will offer to thee the sacrifice of thanksgiving, And will call upon the name of Jehovah.

Ephesians 5:1-2

1. Be ye therefore imitators of God, as beloved children; 2. and walk in love, even as Christ also loved you, and gave himself up for us, an offering and a sacrifice to God for an odor of a sweet smell.

Hebrews 13:5

5. Through him then let us offer up a sacrifice of praise to God continually, that is, the fruit of lips which make confession to his name.

#3. BOW DOWN (*BAROUCH*) *[BAR ROO K]*

Genesis 18:1-2

1. And Jehovah appeared unto him by the oaks of Mamre, as he sat in the tent door in the heat of the day. 2. And he lifted up his eyes and looked, and, lo, three men stood over against him. And when he saw them, he ran to meet them from the tent door, and bowed himself to the earth,

#4. PLAYING INSTRUMENTS (*ZAMAR*) *[ZE MAR]*

Psalms 150

1. Praise ye Jehovah. Praise God in his sanctuary: Praise him in the firmament of his power. 2. Praise him for his mighty acts: Praise him according to his excellent greatness. 3. Praise him with trumpet sound: Praise him with psaltery and harp. 4. Praise him with timbrel and dance: Praise him with stringed instruments and pipe. 5. Praise him with loud cymbals: Praise him with high sounding cymbals. 6. Let everything that hath breath praise Jehovah. Praise ye Jehovah.

#5. SHOUT (*SHABACH*) *[SHA BACK]*

Leviticus 9

22. And Aaron lifted up his hands toward the people, and blessed them; and he came down from offering the sin-offering, and the burnt-offering, and the peace-offerings. 23. And Moses and Aaron went into the tent of meeting, and came out, and blessed the people: and the glory of Jehovah appeared unto all the people.

Psalms 32

10. Be glad in Jehovah, and rejoice, ye righteous; And shout for joy, all ye that are upright in heart.

#6. DANCE (*HALELL*) *[HA LAUL]*

2 Samuel 6

14. And David danced before Jehovah with all his might; and David was girded with a linen ephod. 15. So David and all the house of Israel brought up the ark of Jehovah with shouting, and with the sound of the trumpet.

Psalms 149

1. Praise ye Jehovah. Sing unto Jehovah a new song, And his praise in the assembly of the saints. 2. Let Israel rejoice in him that made him: Let the children of Zion be joyful in their King. 3. Let them praise his name in the dance: Let them sing praises unto him with timbrel and harp. 4. For Jehovah taketh pleasure in his people: He will beautify the meek with salvation. 5. Let the saints exult in glory: Let them sing for joy upon their beds. 6. Let the high praises of God be in their mouth, And a two-edged sword in their hand; 7. To execute vengeance upon the nations, And punishments upon the peoples; 8. To bind their kings with chains, And their nobles with fetters of iron; 9. To execute upon them the judgment written: This honor have all his saints. Praise ye Jehovah.

#7. DOING ALL SIX, AT SAME TIME (*TEHILLAH*) *[TA HEAL A]* *HIGHEST FORM OF PRAISE AND WORSHIP!!!*

Tehillah is when we reach that place where we get lost in our Praise and Worship. It is when we get lost in Him. When we forget about the stress of life and we focus only on His Greatness! Tehillah is the combination of singing, clapping, shouting, dancing, and rejoicing before the Lord.

Pastor Howard preaching at the Christian-Hebrew Shabach Service

THE BIBLE

*P*icture this; you have spent your life raised in a single parent home, with your mother. She did such a great job, working two jobs day and night and still making time for you. Your father was killed in an accident before you were born and you never knew him. For thirty years you've wondered what he was really like, and if he could speak with you what would he say? What advice would he give to you? How would he show you his love? Then you find a book that he wrote to you the day before he died. In it he tells you his most intimate thoughts, shares advice with you about life, and shares with you his favorite songs, poems, and stories. He demonstrates such love for you even before you were born! The book was literally a love letter to you from your father!

Now ask yourself, what would you do with the book? How often would you read it? Would it become one of your most valuable possessions? What would it be worth to you? Would it be priceless? As you may have guessed by now, I'm referencing the Bible.

The Bible is God's love letter to His Children. Our heavenly Father wrote us a love letter telling us about Himself, giving us direction for life, and filled it with His favorite songs, poems, and stories. He demonstrates such love for you and I; He tells us that He loved us even before we were born! God desires an intimate, personal relationship with us. We are His children, and God has made Himself available to us in so many ways. One of the ways is to study and learn His Word (the Bible)! It sickens me to see how ignorant Christians are in reference to the Bible. I once read a survey that said Christians read the Bible about 4-hours per week and watch TV about 28-hours per week. If that's true, then we are watching TV seven times more than were reading God's Word! So is it fair to say that as a nation we are listening to Hollywood seven times more than were listening to God? It's no wonder this country is in the shape it's in! To see this nation turned around, I believe that Christians must begin to read God's Word more and fall in love with God all over again!

The Bible is more than just a book. It's more than just a history document, and it's more than just a map or a travel guide to Heaven. The Bible is alive or a Living Word; it's God speaking to us here and now! Our Bible gives us information about God and allows us to discover His personality. The scripture compares God's Word to a mirror. You look into the mirror to see yourself as you really are. As a born again believer studies God's Word, through the power of the Holy Spirit, you see yourself as you really are, spiritually.

James 1:22-24 -- *²²But be ye doers of the word, and not hearers only, deceiving your own selves. ²³For if any be a hearer of the word, and not a doer, he is like*

unto a man beholding his natural face in a glass:
²⁴For he beholdeth himself, and goeth his way, and
straightway forgetteth what manner of man he was.

I believe that our wrong attitudes, broken relationships, harmful habits, and sinful nature all become obvious in the mirror of God's Word. The believer who does not act on God's instructions, but goes away unchanged, is like a person who looks in the mirror and immediately forgets what he or she looks like.

The Land of the Ducks

I read a story once about an imaginary land of ducks… ok, stay with me. Every Sunday the ducks of the land would waddle to church, the Duck Pastor would quack out a sermon to the ducks. He would say "Ducks, you have wings" and all of the ducks would quack amen. Then he would say "Ducks, you can fly like the eagles and soar high in the air…" and again all of the ducks would quack amen. Then after church all of the ducks would waddle back home.

This is an example of Christians today. They waddle to church each Sunday carrying all of their problems and afflictions. They hear the preacher say "You can mount up with wings like eagles and run and not grow weary…." They amen him and waddle home still carrying the same problems and afflictions they came in with. Sunday after Sunday, week after week. Without proper grounding in the Word of God Christians can't understand just who they are in Christ Jesus!

God gave us the Bible to show us:
• How He feels toward us.
• How we should live.

91

- What priorities we should have in life.
- How to get along with and relate to one another and how to relate to Him.

In a nutshell, the Bible is our spiritual food! In life if we go a few days without food what happens? We die! The same is true with our spiritual life. If we continue to go without eating spiritual food or reading the Bible we grow spiritually tired and eventually die! Here are some ways to eat God's Word and grow strong and healthy spiritually.

- Read the Bible with the purpose of finding something to apply to your life.
- Read the Bible a little bit EVERY DAY!
- Discipline yourself to follow a plan on how you're going to read the Bible. And stick with your plan!
- Read book by book (You can start with the Gospels and then go to Acts, Romans, and let the Holy Spirit lead you.)
- Memorize scriptures.
- Worship and pray before and after reading the Bible.

The Bible isn't in a chronological order but there is an order to how the Bible is arranged! The first 5 books, or the **Pentateuch or Torah,** is God dealing with humanity from the start of creation; Adam, Eve, Abraham, the Israelites, the Law and Ceremonies. Next are the **Books of History:** they tell how God was with His people, the Israelites, as they conquered their land, set up their nation, and then are taken captive and lived in captivity, and eventually returned to their land. Following the Books of History are **The Wisdom Books:** these are poems, songs, psalms, hymns and heartfelt emotions from relationship with God. These books are filled with Godly wisdom about life and love! **The Books of the Prophets** follow: these books warned Israel about the consequences of turning their back on God. They also predicted the birth of Jesus, the life and death of Jesus, and other future events. The Old Testament points to the coming Messiah – Jesus.

Now let's look at the order of the New Testament. Starting with the **Gospels:** these are the accounts of the life and teaching of Jesus, His birth, life, death, and His amazing resurrection! The New testament Church was set up in the book of **Acts.** This book tells how the Christian Church began and spread through the world. Following Acts, we read **The Books of Letters.** These are writings of the Apostles and the early Christian leaders. They teach on beliefs, behavior, relationship with God, and our relationship with other people. We end our New Testament with the great **Book of Revelation.** This book, written by an older John, reviews human history, and its final end, God's promises to us and life beyond this world. This book gives humanity a glimpse into Heaven and eternity.

I hope this has helped you in your quest to read your Bible and learn more about the God we serve. Below are some scriptures that may help you through some of the storms of life.

- **Impatient:** Philippians 4:6-7
- **Lonely:** Matthew 28-20
- **Fear:** 2 Timothy 1:7 / 1 Peter 3:12-14
- **Discouraged:** Romans 8
- **Difficult times:** 2 Corinthians 1:8-11
- **Sick or suffering:** Romans 5:1-5
- **Tempted:** Hebrews 4:14-16

BLESSED TIMES
TWO

I cried out to God at an early age, that He would give me many things,
Fame and Fortune became my hearts desire, from the inside I knew that I would go higher,
I measured success with my thoughts in my mind, but God showed me my blessings are given according to His time.
Many blessings were mine from the Word I knew,
But now I realize that as a child of God, I'm blessed..... Times two.

*T*he first blessing came to me when I was a young man; she was delivered to me by my Creator's hand.
I thought I knew how to love but to my surprise, it was the unspeakable love when I saw my own eyes,
When I held my blessing in my arms, I knew that I could never let her go
Now I cry out again "Oh Lord" for the Blessed has blessed me so.

So many blessings are mine, from the Word I knew
But now I realize that as a child of God I'm
blessed….. Times two.

*T*he second blessing came to me in the most
unusual form,
As calm as the first one was the next came as a
violent storm,
It is said that the Lord gives and the Lord takes
away,
But it was unto the Lord that my heart cried out
that day,
As a father, and as a dad, losing my blessing filled
my heart with fear,
But on the day my blessing was restored back I
stood as a man with eyes full of tears.

*N*ow I know what blessings are, from the Word
that I thought I knew,
And I stand here before you today as a man who is
truly blessed ….Times two!!!

MY first Blessing
was Hannah and
the Lord blessed
me again with
Kaitie! Both are
Daddy's Girls! I
am truly a dad
…Blessed Times Two!!!

CHRISTMAS - JUST
ANOTHER DAY?

*L*et us take a long look at our world that is so
confused, about a holiday that is so misused!
Christmas!!! The birth of our Christ.
It's misused as another winter selling device.
Walk down the streets, and look into our stores.
The gimmicks and Santa Claus pack the floors.
Christians, it's time to make our move… spiritually
speaking, let us put our lives back in God's groove.
Let the knowledge of Christ rule, and it will take us
higher in this world of jewels.
Take heed of the word that I send. The ignorance of
His people must come to an end!
And NEVER will the people say, "Christmas is just
another day."
You see, our society is functioning without reason,
because without Jesus Christ there would be no
season!
So I wrote this rhyme for everyone.
It's about the Messiah, the Christ, the Son…

He's the Son of the living God and the Prince of Peace.

He was born to die to fulfill a lease.

This all happened in a city named Bethlehem, on Christmas day came the Son of Man.

And on that same night at a place afar, the Spirit from Heaven descended as a star.

A group of shepherds watched their flocks by night, and out of the sky appeared a bright light.

The thunder rolled out a great voice from an angel named Gabriel saying, "REJOICE!"

"Born to you this day is a Savior, a Son and a King, so celebrate and let the whole world sing!!!"

Luke 2 - The Greatest Gift of All!

GIVE UP?

*N*ever give up! That is what they said.
So I move forward down the road of fate.
The wind begins to blow; I feel the fear in the air.
What will happen from this point on? Will I live or die? Can I move on?
My body is tired. My flesh is weak. My mind says to stop, but my heart tells me to press on.
So I once again I start to move.
Is my destiny to fail? Can I become more than I look on the surface?
My skin is dry and the winds from the storm are now overtaking me. I'm ready to give up and lay down in the bed of defeat.
I have no strength left; I have nothing else to give. My body is tired. My flesh is weak. My mind says to stop, but my heart tells me to press on.
So I once again I start to move.
No where to go, no one to lean on, no where to turn, no one to love, nothing to believe in… I can't hold on much longer; my grip softens.

And then right at the very moment that I was to let go I saw it!

It was a hand reaching out for me. As I touched the hand, I can't explain it, but something touched me. Now because of the hand I know who I am and I see what I can do!

I am created by the Great I AM, in His image.

I am great because greatness lives inside of me!

I can do all things because He who is in me has already given me the strength to do so!

Give up? It is no longer an option!

**I can do all things through
Christ who strengthens me.
Philippians 4:13**

THE WALK

*T*rapped / Ensnared / Enthralled / I'm Captive to myself.
I walk through the valley; it's dark, cold, and frightening.
My spirit is weary; I grow more tired with each step. My breath is weak.
I feel like an animal snared in a cage.
The world watches, and awaits the day that I will become free. But free from what, or free from whom?
I count the minutes and the minutes slowly become days, the days become weeks, and weeks become years.
I know what is expected of me, but I grow hungry. I thirst.
So I take my seat at the table of darkness and I begin to eat.
I want to resist the desires of my flesh but I'm trapped.
I'm Held Captive / Enslaved / Caged / Confined.

Once I could see clearly, but now I'm blinded by the fog. Once I could hear, but now I hear no more. There was a time that I could feel, I could love, and I could be loved.

Now the coldness that I fought so hard against rules me. I'm wounded, and my wounds begin to bleed.

I'm an animal, snared in a cage.

My hope that I carry is the hope that there will be a day, a day when I reach out for you, a day that I call you, and a day you answer.

I long for the day that I see your face once again, feel your touch, and hear your voice calling my name.

I now approach the bottom of yet another mountain. I have no strength left to climb.

Tired and weary I stop. I lay myself down on the ground and ponder these final thoughts;

Can I love? Am I loved? Only the right answer to these ever so important questions can move me on.

I long for the day that I see your face once again, feel your touch, and hear your voice calling my name.

So I walk on!

"There is a dying world outside walking and searching for a love. Only the love of the Creator can heal them and give them the strength to press on. The Creator's love is displayed through our actions. Who do you know that's searching for that unconditional love that we freely carry? Freely we've been given and freely we must learn to give."

Pastor Howard

HER DADDY

*W*here is my daddy? Where has he gone?
As I cry myself to sleep, I've never felt so alone.

Sometimes late at night I awake from my dream,
I swear I feel his touch, my tears flow like a
stream.
I remember when I was young; he would hold me
for hours on end.
What I would do to hear his voice, to be in his arms
once again.

Where is my daddy? Where has he gone?
As I cry myself to sleep, I've never felt so alone.

My daddy stood so tall; he was a man among men.
So rough on the outside, yet so gentle and loving
within.
He would tuck me in late at night with butterfly
kisses on my cheek,
Oh, how I miss those kisses, broken hearted I stand
and weep.

Where is my daddy? Where has he gone?
As I cry myself to sleep, I've never felt so alone.

He gave me his eyes, and his values I will never leave.
Dwelling on thoughts about him, suddenly an inner peace I receive.
Daddy showed me how to live through the joy of God's Holy Spirit,
And he introduced me to his Heavenly Daddy, now being alone – I'll never fear it.

Where is my daddy? He's with God in Heavenly Grace, and soon his little girl will be with him with butterfly kisses on her face.
I know where my daddy is, I know where he's gone. I've now stopped crying myself to sleep, for I now know — I'll never be alone!

God is the Father to the fatherless. God is the Daddy to those who have no dad; God is the mother to those who have no mother. He's your brother, your sister, your wife, your husband, the one who will never let you down and the one who will never leave you! God is the only one that a grieving heart can find comfort in! He is our Father and we are His Children!

JOY

*A*s a Christian "Joy" should be displayed at all times! But unfortunately, a lot of times Christians are some of the unhappiest people. There is nothing worse than a puckered, pickled-faced Christian trying to sell the Joy of the Holy Ghost. The world is sad and angry and looking for Joy; we have the Joy they're looking for!

What does the Bible say about Joy? Joy is one of the fruits of the Spirit. *"But the fruit of the Spirit is love, joy, peace, patience, kindness, goodness, faith, gentleness, and self-control. Against such things there is no law"* (Galatians 5:22-23). So, is it fair to say that if we have the Spirit of God in us then we should also display the fruits of the Spirit?

One definition I read said that Joy is "a strong feeling of happiness; gladness; delight." It's a state of contentment or satisfaction. Joy is anything that causes delight or gladness or being blessed. We who have been saved from darkness are blessed! We need to show it! Let's make a commitment to God and ourselves that in the future that we will display the fruit of JOY wherever we go!

I love it when I'm stopped in stores by folks and am asked how I stay so happy. People ask me all of the time how I keep a smile on my face. I just smile and answer, "God gave me dimples, and I intend to use them." The next time you go out, make it a point to keep a smile on your face and watch how folks respond.

"The Joy of the Lord will be my Strength!"

SPIRITUAL LAMB

*A*s God looked upon a region, with nowhere to turn,
So many questions, so much to learn.
Years of bondage and years of fear,
A generation was crying a river of tears.
Nothing good could ever happen in this place of forsaken,
No one wanted to stay, if we could only escape.
Could anyone help? Would anyone understand?
The Lord smiled down and said, "I'll send a lamb!"

*W*ho was this lamb shepherd sent to watch over God's sheep?
He carried a unique sound, a drum of a different beat.
The words that he spoke erupted as fire,
The vision inside Him burned with desire.
But was the resistance too strong? Would it put Him down?

Could He stand against the wind, could He hold
His ground?
Then a voice came from the heavens and said "You
must understand...
I have sent unto you My only Son, a visionary, a
lamb."

Then the days of the storms came and there were
days of war,
But this man from God stood tall, knowing whom
He was fighting for!
The resistance hit hard, and brought every weapon
forth,
But time after time the resistance was taken by
force.
You see, He's a man on a mission, and His mission
is clear.
To bring a Word of freedom to a people, who are
living in fear.
So today let's rise behind Him, and let us take a
stand.
Let us move forward with the Word of God, with
Jesus, the true spiritual lamb.

A Word From God

God is about to do something, in this area that's never
been done.
He's raising up a body of believers who know how
to overcome!
Church get ready for the future, for the blessing of
the kingdom is about to flow into a blessed church,
standing on the city gates, reaping a harvest, from
over the years we have sowed!

We will become a family, and at the head, will be our Heavenly Dad...
Who will love us and lead us into a land of plenty.
Church, this is the time to move into our promised land!!!! So today as we take a step into our future, and hear from Jehovah, our God who's the Great I Am,
I invite you to join me, as I thank Him, for being my Heavenly Father, our spiritual lamb.

STARFISH

Someone once told a story about an old man, walking on the beach at dawn who noticed a young boy ahead of him picking up starfish and flinging them into the sea. Catching up with the youth, he asked the boy what he was doing. The answer was that the stranded starfish would die if left in the morning sun. "But the beach goes on for miles and miles, and there are millions of starfish," countered the man. "How can your effort make any difference?" The young boy looked at the starfish in his hand and then threw it to safety in the waves as he said, "It makes a difference to this one."

**Evangelism is winning the world
for Jesus, one starfish at a time...**

SAY WHAT?

"God is bringing you out to bring you in...He will bring you down to pick you up..."

*T*his was actually a quote a man once said in a church from the pulpit. I have no idea what he as talking about, and I'll bet he didn't either.

"God is qualifying you to be qualified; when He qualifies you the world will know you're qualified!"

This was another quote an evangelist said at church from the pulpit. He shouted it with his best charismatic voice, and most of the folks in the congregation shouted amen. One person looked at me and said "that's deep." It wasn't deep; it was jibber jabber that made no sense. We must be careful what we say in church and what we put God's name on. Time and time again I have heard preachers preach for an hour and say nothing.

Sometimes preachers and Christians feel that they need to say all of this "spiritual jibber jabber" to look good. Well that's pride! I end with this; weigh everything out that is said, receive what is from God and throw the rest away!

XV

THE ONE

*O*ne day God wanted to bless one of His children.
So He asked all of His Children, that's anyone and
everyone, to become a blessing. It was a small
blessing, a small task and anyone could have done it.
Everyone thought someone else would do it; after all
it was God who asked. Someone was going to do it,
everyone had intentions to it, and again any one could
have done it; but no one did it!

No one dreamed that everyone would wait for
someone else to do it and someone even once started
it, but no one finished it. This simple task to bless
one of God's children, a task that could have, would
have, and should have been done by anyone and
everyone, was done by no one because everyone
seemed to be waiting on someone else to do it and no
one did it! No one did what someone, anyone, and
everyone could have, would have, and should have
done!

Know this: God has called anyone and everyone to become a someone, through Jesus. Through this calling, this new and born again someone has been commissioned to become a blessing to anyone and everyone throughout the whole world!

So today I preach to anyone and everyone and specifically to the one someone that the Blessed One, Sanctified One, Righteous One, Divine One, and True Heavenly One by the Word of the only Son and through the power of the Holy One is ready to bless you today!

HEALING RAIN

The Word of the Lord is:
The Drought Will End And the Rain Will Come!!

James 5:13-18 KJV

13. Is any among you afflicted? let him pray. Is any merry? let him sing psalms. 14. Is any sick among you? let him call for the elders of the church; and let them pray over him, anointing him with oil in the name of the Lord: 15. And the prayer of faith shall save the sick, and the Lord shall raise him up; and if he have committed sins, they shall be forgiven him. 16. Confess your faults one to another, and pray one for another, that ye may be healed. The effectual fervent prayer of a righteous man availeth much. 17. Elias was a man subject to like passions as we are, and he prayed earnestly that it might not rain: and it rained not on the earth by the space of three years and six months. 18. And he prayed again, and the heaven gave rain, and the earth brought forth her fruit.

So many times I have talked with and ministered to Christians who are in such a dry place in their lives. I hear people saying "I just feel spiritually dry" or "I'm just waiting for the Lord to do something for me." So many of us spend our lives worshiping God as if He was a Santa Clause, ready to hear our wish list and then we leave Him until next year or at least the next disaster in our lives. And we wonder why our spiritual lives are dried up.

I Hear The Sound Of Rain From Heaven

God has spoken to me that in these days He is, as the scripture says, "going to pour out His Spirit, His Love, His Compassion, and His Grace on ALL FLESH!" I now speak to His people all over the world and say that "the seasons of spiritual drought are coming to an end and the Rain of the Holy Spirit is about ready to fall upon His Church like never before!"

In 1 Kings 17 and 18, we read that the world was in a dry place. We meet a man of God named Elijah (Elijah represents the Word of God!) Elijah (The Word of God) said that there was going to be a drought! Note that the devil didn't produce the drought, but it was the Word of God that sent the drought! Sometimes God will allow you to go into a dry season, but remember it's just a DRY SEASON! A season is just for a short time. Seasons will come and seasons will go. Even in a spiritually dry season we always need to know that "God's Rain is on its way!!!"

The first Word from Elijah was that God was going to send a drought. Now thereafter a New Word is manifesting from the Heavens! In our walk with God, remember spiritual droughts are only for a season and there is a new Word from God. The new Word God said is, "I will now allow the rain to fall on the ground." This drought that you're facing may have afflicted you for a season, but this time tomorrow you should know that "Me and my house will be filled with joy and peace from heaven and we will be dancing in the rain; God's heavenly rain!"

Fighting For What You Believe In

When God told Elijah that the rain was on the way, the man of God had to take a stand. In Chapter 18, we read about how he faced the 450 prophets of Baal and the 400 prophets of Asherah. They tested their gods, then the man of God said to move out of the way and let me show you the real power of a true and living God!!!

There is a dying world longing to see the true healing power of the GOD of glory! As a world is crying out, it seems that Christians spend most of their time walking around in their own world and doing nothing for God's Kingdom. Then we wonder why we are not experiencing the fullness of God's power!

In our text, right in the middle of the drought, God asks Elijah to do the unthinkable: God commands Elijah to pour water on the altar. Sometimes when you're in a drought God will ask you to give the same thing that you are asking for... If you're in a financial drought, then give! According to the book of Luke "Give and it will be given back....." If you're in a marital drought then pour your marriage on the altar! If you're in a health drought, then now is the time to pour yourself out on the altar and receive God's eternal healing; GOD'S Healing Rain!

"I Hear the Sound of Rain from Heaven…"
LET IT RAIN!!!

After Elijah prophesied, "the rain is on the way" he and his servant went to Mt. Carmel. (Mt Carmel - a fruitful and plentiful place.) They got out of the valley that they were in and went to a new place, a land of plenty! Then as we read "the sky opens up and out of a small cloud (shaped as a man's hand) the rain comes just as the Word of God said."

NOW SAY TO YOURSELF:

IF I AM GOING TO COME OUT OF MY SPIRITUAL DROUGHT, I NEED TO HAVE THE FAITH THAT THE SMALLEST CLOUD, THE SMALLEST SEED OF FAITH, CAN PRODUCE THE MIGHTIEST STORM -- A GREAT BLESSING FROM MY GOD.

"I Hear the Sound of Rain from Heaven…"
LET IT RAIN!!!

XV

LOCAL CHURCH

I've been thinking about the *local church* and her role in our day to day faith walk. The Church was established to help Christian brothers and sisters deal with daily problems Christ-like. The Bible says the Church was founded upon two basic principles:
1. Ministering, one to another.
2. Fellowshipping one with another.

Lately, there has been a nationwide movement to destroy the local church and/or downplay her involvement in our spiritual walk. I have read internet blogs, national articles and different publications basically stating that we no longer need the local church!

I will stand and be the first to say this is false teaching and couldn't be more wrong! The book of Hebrews 10:25 says, *"Not forsaking the assembling of ourselves together, as the manner of some is; but exhorting one another: and so much the more, as ye see the day approaching."* I believe that the local church, under God-ordained leadership, is necessary in the life of the Christian.

People ask, "Were there local churches in the New Testament?" YES! As you read the New Testament you will find that many of the Epistles were literal letters to a local church or local churches: Corinth, Galatia, Ephesus, Philippi, Colosse, and Thessalonica… Seven more churches were addressed in Revelation 2 & 3: Ephesus, Smyrna, Pergamum, Thyatira, Sardis, Philadelphia, and Laodicea… Acts talks about local churches; an example would be the Church at Jerusalem - Acts 8:1, Acts 11:22 and the Church at Antioch - Acts 13:1!

I heard on Christian radio that some Christians now believe that the Internet is an acceptable replacement for the local church; this grieved me, because I know how wrong that is! One person said there is no real Jesus in church. I beg to differ; Jesus is in you and the church should be made up of you, so you are to bring Jesus to the church meetings… (If there is no Jesus at church, then maybe the problem is... you.) Now, I understand that some folks are restricted to home due to illnesses and physically can't get out to church, and this is the time when believers should bring church to them. Time and time again folks tell me about a bad experience they may have had at church, so that's their excuse for not going to church. I've said it before and I'll say it again "There is no excuse for not being part of a local church. Missing church or not being involved in your local church should be *No Option*! Find a local church and a local Pastor and get involved. Be blessed by becoming a blessing!!!

Not forsaking the assembling of ourselves together, as the manner of some is; but exhorting one another: and so much the more, as ye see the day approaching. Hebrews 10:25

FAITH LIFESTYLE

*H*ello all. We had a great Wednesday night Bible study last night. I'm teaching a series on Faith Lifestyle... (James in the Bible). I talked about how due to a lack of "Faith Lifestyle" (not a lack of faith, but a lack of "Faith Lifestyle") we become roller coaster Christians... up one day and bottomed out the next. It's only a "Faith Lifestyle" that can stop this cycle. We have too many believers on this cycle, and when they're on the mountaintop it's great, but when they hit the valleys of life they fall apart. It's the "Faith Lifestyle" that teaches us that "Location doesn't matter!!!" David said, "*If* I make my bed in hell You are with me..." (Psalms 139). He also said, "I can walk through the valley of the shadow of death and You are with me..." (Psalms 23).

I believe God wants to take His people to a place of "Faith Lifestyle." Let me explain. Christian faith is believing in God and knowing Jesus is the Son of God, etc. All of that is great, but a "Lifestyle of Faith" teaches us that the same faith that "Knowing God is

God," is the same faith that will get us through those long and hard times and days.

We can have faith in end times and faith in Heaven, but can we have faith that we know that God will make me have a great day TODAY, regardless of circumstances... TODAY regardless of conditions... TODAY regardless of situations. That's a "Faith Lifestyle." It's more than just pretending to be holy or spiritually deep. It's more than just speaking out faith words or verses. It's more than just blogging some thoughts and trying to convince everyone that you're a faith person. It's more than carrying your Bible around or wearing Christian clothing or jewelry.

It's living day by day by faith - faith that God will take you places each and every day. Faith that God will show you freat things each and every day. Faith that God will not only get you through, but faith that He will walk you from the beginning to end and even during the hard times you will have a peace and a joy that surpasses any and all understanding (Philippians 4:7).

It's that "Faith Lifestyle" that the early Church walked in. It's that "Faith Lifestyle" that the Disciples and Apostles walked in. And it's that "Faith Lifestyle" that will take us to a realm where we will see great things from God's kingdom, including signs, wonders, and miracles. The choice is ours; we can live the way we've been living and receive the same results, or we can make a change in 2009 and choose to make our Lifestyle a "Faith Lifestyle."

PATIENCE VS. IMPATIENCE

*H*ave you ever noticed that when you feel like you've made it, or you feel like you finally got it together, all hell breaks loose? The Bible teaches many lessons about patience. Patience is described as a spiritual gift that can only be developed through trials and tribulations. A few synonyms for patience are: endurance, staying power, stamina, open-mindedness, charity, serenity, and tolerance. It's amazing that when we read about patience, and the total package that comes with it, we really don't see the contemporary Christian faith. We as Christians spend so much time picking out the faults and imperfections of our Christian brothers and sisters, and so little time looking for good in everyone and finding God's will in each situation.

During times of stretching when we're in the wilderness, we are often confronted with different circumstances and situations that test our patience. Remember, patience can only be developed through trials and tribulations. I have noticed through my spiritual walk, that it's during these times that we are quick to take on different offences. Someone once said that the word "offence" literally means "bait." Think about it, the enemy uses offences to bait us into a trap and lure us away from God and His Will for our lives. Offence is the antonym or the opposite of patience. You see, when we are baited into an offence, we do not have charity, love, tolerance, or any other gift that is developed through patience.

Over the past month, I have been involved in two different situations in my personal life that required patience and the gifts that fall under it. I would love to write a great testimony about how God just moved through me and how great I handled each situation. But, if I said that then I would be lying. I was baited into an offence and said things both times that I walked away wondering why and saying to myself, "I know better than that!" Does this sound familiar? In both situations, I feel that the other person was at fault, I was right and my stance was Biblically correct, but my attitude was wrong. I have come to discover that, *"ALL OF THE RIGHT IN THE WORLD, WITH A BAD ATTITUDE IS JUST WRONG!"*

Well, for those of you who thought I was perfect, you need to wake up, you have never been more wrong. But praise God for grace! I have said many times that there was only one who was Perfect, Righteous, and Just; and they crucified Him! So my blog today is two-fold; first, don't take the bait in times of conflict. Don't let the enemy trap you and lure you in. Secondly, when you stumble and fall (not if, but when, no one's perfect) don't beat yourself up over it or allow others to tear you down. Remember, we all have imperfections, faults, and shortcomings; we all mess up. Occasionally, we all choose to do the wrong thing or go the wrong way, or have a wrong attitude, amen? Let's learn to give each other a break, and God will develop true spiritual patience in us, that we may be a light into the world and shine before all men!!!

Romans 15:4 KJV
For whatsoever things were written aforetime were written for our learning, that we through patience and comfort of the scriptures might have hope.

1 Timothy 6:11 KJV
But thou, O man of God, flee these things; and follow after righteousness, godliness, faith, love, patience, meekness.

James 1:3 KJV
Knowing this, that the trying of your faith worketh patience.

James 1:4 KJV
But let patience have her perfect work, that ye may be perfect and entire, wanting nothing.

James 5:7 KJV
Be patient therefore, brethren, unto the coming of the Lord. Behold, the husbandman waiteth for the precious fruit of the earth, and hath long patience for it, until he receive the early and latter rain.

James 5:10 KJV
Take, my brethren, the prophets, who have spoken in the name of the Lord, for an example of suffering affliction, and of patience.

XV

THE BOOK OF JAMES

I have been studying the book of James for about two months now. WOW! What an eye-opening experience. I said to a parishioner the other day that I feel like God has been dissecting me. This "spiritual dissecting" isn't a comfortable thing, but it is necessary to perfect me through Christ. Let me explain. We are born with all of this sinful junk inside of us called "original sin." When we become saved, we still have sin in our lives; through salvation it becomes "forgiven sin." For many years now Christians have been taught to walk around pretending this sin wasn't there. So instead of dealing with it, we tend to hide it and pray that nobody ever finds it. Well eventually, what has been hidden is surfaced! Amen? The book of James teaches us how to deal with this sinful nature within ourselves and in others.

The book starts off by teaching us that when we are tempted, TURN TO GOD (James chapter 1:1-27). Notice I said, when we are temped, not if. We are all tempted to do wrong, remember it's our nature. The task at hand is to learn to destroy our nature and follow God's Nature. James chapter two instructs us not to favor rich people over poor. WOW, what a lesson for today's church! This chapter goes on to teach us that our actions demonstrate our faith. Let me be very clear, our salvation is FREE. Jesus paid the price for us, and you will NEVER have to work to earn your spot in Heaven. Just receive the gift of Jesus from God the Father. But it's our day to day actions that will build or destroy our faith and our testimony to others! Remember, it is not always what you say but most of the time the true testimony comes from what you're doing and who you're being.

Next, James teaches us how to speak wisely and the power of the tongue....

James 3:9-12, God's Word

9 With our tongues we praise our Lord and Father. Yet, with the same tongues we curse people, who were created in God's likeness. 10 Praise and curses come from the same mouth. My brothers and sisters, this should not happen! 11 Do clean and polluted water flow out of the same spring? 12 My brothers and sisters, can a fig tree produce olives? Can a grapevine produce figs? In the same way, a pool of salt water can't produce fresh water.

The biggest lie that the devil ever sold us is the proverb that says, "Sticks and stones will break my bones but words will never hurt me." Over the past years I have ministered to so many individuals that had been attacked with words. Our tongue is like a two-edged sword that slices both ways. Let's learn to watch what we say and how we say it. The book of James goes on to talk about how to deal with each other and how to address conflicts in a Godly manner. And I love that way the book ends, by instructing us to be patient at all times.

James 5:7-9 God's Word

7 Brothers and sisters, be patient until the Lord comes again. See how farmers wait for their precious crops to grow. They wait patiently for fall and spring rains. 8 You, too, must be patient. Don't give up hope. The Lord will soon be here. 9 Brothers and sisters, stop complaining about each other, or you will be condemned. Realize that the judge is standing at the door.

I hope today's blog has whet your appetite to read the book of James. But more so, I pray that the Holy Spirit will continue to guide us and teach us to live God-centered lives until we get to eternity!

WHY NOT HERE?

Acts 2:1-4 KJV
Coming of the Holy Spirit

1And when the day of Pentecost was fully come, they were all with one accord in one place. 2And suddenly there came a sound from heaven as of a rushing mighty wind, and it filled all the house where they were sitting. 3And there appeared unto them cloven tongues like as of fire, and it sat upon each of them. 4And they were all filled with the Holy Ghost, and began to speak with other tongues, as the Spirit gave them utterance.

If it happened there; then I ask why not here. And if it happened then, I ask why not NOW? I believe that the first steps to a real Holy Spirit Outpouring are as follows. #1. The folks have got to be together in one accord! There can be **no separation** by color, sex, or religious barriers. #2. Let the 500 become 120. It's ok, the 3000 are waiting! Don't be afraid when folks leave, they're not really with you anyway. God has an army of people who will stand with you and for you as you seek God's will. #3. Don't be afraid to wait for it, even when others are leaving, wait! #4. Be prepared and ready to be blessed.

Acts 2:12-21 KJV

12And they were all amazed, and were in doubt, saying one to another, What meaneth this? 13Others mocking said, These men are full of new wine. 14But Peter, standing up with the eleven, lifted up his voice, and said unto them, Ye men of Judaea, and all ye that dwell at Jerusalem, be this known unto you, and hearken to my words: 15For these are not drunken, as ye suppose, seeing it is but the third hour of the day. 16But this is that which was spoken by the prophet Joel; 17And it shall come to pass in the last days, saith God, I will pour out of my Spirit upon all flesh: and your sons and your daughters shall prophesy, and your young men shall see visions, and your old men shall dream dreams: 18And on my servants and on my handmaidens I will pour out in those days of my Spirit; and they shall prophesy: 19And I will shew wonders in heaven above, and signs in the earth beneath; blood, and fire, and vapour of smoke: 20The sun shall be turned into darkness, and the moon into blood, before the great and notable day of the Lord come: 21And it shall come to pass, that whosoever shall call on the name of the Lord shall be saved.

Again, if it happened there; then I ask why not here. And if it happened then, I ask, why not NOW? In Acts 2, the Heavens opened up and God poured out His Spirit upon ALL FLESH!!!! So why is today's church not experiencing the same? I ask, why not here in Philippi, WV? Why not here at an old skating rink called Haven of Hope? Why not here with a group of average, normal people who love their God? I say, God if You can do it then and there, then why not *here* and *now*?

Some may say, "Why or how could God show up in nowhere - Philippi, WV?" Well, let's look at Holy Spirit history in America. It was May 2, 1870 and two former slaves named Simon Seymour (also known as Simon Simon) and Phillis Salabar, who lived in Centerville, Louisiana, had a son. They were just ordinary black folk who were freed from slavery and really had no special or supernatural qualities. Just regular folks like us! The two named their newborn son, their first child, William Joseph Seymour. It was said that the family was beyond dirt poor. The dad had gotten malaria from the southern swamps after joining President Lincoln's army to fight for his people's freedom, and the mother's personal property was valued at 55-cents when she died.

William Seymour also suffered the injustice and prejudice of the reconstruction south. Violence against freedman was common, and groups like the Ku Klux Klan terrorized southern Louisiana. This one-eyed black man, named William J Seymour, was from many different religions; his parents were married by a Methodist preacher, he was baptized by a Catholic priest, and a Baptist minister preached his parents funereal. Seymour attended a black freedman school in Centerville, and learned to read and write. He later became a Methodist preacher. Soon, however, he joined the Church of God Reformation movement.

God had healed Seymour from a near fatal bout with smallpox; the illness left him blind in one eye and scarred his face. But he wore the scars as hope that God brought him back to life for a reason... He would later find that reason as he walked into a converted warehouse where a group of believers were having prayer meetings!

The date was now April 1906, in that old empty warehouse located at 312 Azusa Street in the industrial district in LA, California. The front page headlines of the LA Times read, "The fire of Pentecost comes to LA on Azusa Street." The believers said "the very atmosphere of Heaven had come down!" Revival from Acts 2 had hit the west coast in the United States of America. One reporter wrote, "That evening would be hard to describe. People fell to the floor as if unconscious; others shouted and ran through the house. One neighbor, Jennie Evans Moore, played the piano, something she did not have the ability to do before. People were speaking in other tongues...." Over the next few days of continuous outpouring, hundreds gathered. The streets were filled and Seymour preached to the streets. In that old, empty warehouse located at 312 Azusa Street in the industrial district in LA, California. In an unfinished building with a low ceiling, a dirt floor, (used as a storage building and stable), and mix matched chairs with wooden planks laid out for a prayer altar, and two wooden crates covered by a cheap cloth used for the pulpit. GOD SHOWED UP!

In a time when strict segregation was the norm in America, white and black families sang and prayed and worshiped together... and a one-eyed, black son of slaves stood up and called forth the power and the glory of GOD! And fire fell from Heaven, and within weeks the warehouse could not contain the people! They came from the north, south, east, and west. Every color -- black and white, men and women, and children alike! Revival fire fell! They spoke and sang in tongues of angels and saw healings and miracles.

Today, over 600-million Spirit-filled Christians trace our roots back to that old empty warehouse, and 36-year old William Joseph Seymour, and the Azusa Street revival.

Now, I say all of that to say this. If it happened there, then I ask, why not *here*? And if it happened then, I ask, why not *now*? When folks get together and are in one accord! No separation by color, sex, or religious barriers... and we can say, "Let the 150 become 60 or 70... it's ok the 3000 are waiting!" God's Holy Spirit will COME in a mighty way. Revival will pour out, and the Heavens will open up! Church, greater days are ahead, be prepared and ready to be blessed!

COMMITMENT

*I*n today's society, the word "commitment" is seen as the ultimate threat. This fear has filtered itself into the Church house and our Christian walk. The word commitment by definition is: *a promise, a pledge, a vow, loyalty, and dedication.* Wow, when you think about it, you can see how the word commitment is a threat to the humanistic society that the U.S. has become. Humanism is being absorbed by secular concerns and self-interest. Christianity is being sold-out and totally dedicated to God and not to self. See the conflict? The Bible teaches us to kill our selfish desires each day, and to renew our commitment to God and to our spiritual calling. But it seems that today's culture has taught us not to be too committed to anyone or anything. What's wrong with us? I ask this. Without commitment, what is our society becoming?

In the religious realm, this lack of or fear of commitment has really had its toll on the local church.

Christians have developed this lazy attitude that "I'll commit to God, and I'll commit to church, as long as it's on my terms." Again, being a Christian is all about God and His terms, not ours!!! If you want to see God move in a mighty way in your life, you must first renew your commitment to Him. Then put to rest these humanistic thoughts that have been leading you down the wrong path.

Ask yourself these questions:

1. Where is the place (church, ministry, etc…) that God has called me to?
2. Am I in the place that He has called me to?
3. What is my commitment to God and the ministry that He has placed me in?
4. How can I be less committed to my human desires and more committed to God's will for my life?
5. How can I be more committed to my local church, my local Pastor, and the folks in need who live in my community?

As you answer these questions, I pray that you would begin to renew your commitment to God, and to your local church and Pastor. As you do, you'll see your walk with God soar to levels that you can only dream of today. As the word commitment may be the ultimate threat to the world; commitment is God's way to empower His children with His divine wisdom. Remember, greater days are ahead!

NATIONAL DAY
OF PRAYER

*T*he **National Day of Prayer** is a day set aside and designated by the U.S. Congress and signed by President Harry S. Truman in 1952, as a day when people are asked to come together and pray for local, state and national government. It was created as a floating holiday in 1952, but set on the first Thursday in May by President Ronald Reagan.

This nation was founded upon Judeo-Christian values, including prayer to God. (Oh yeah, that's Jehovah God, not just any old god.) In 1775, the Continental Congress asked the colonies to pray for wisdom in forming our nation!!! I read a story about a reporter coming into a joint session of the U.S. Congress and looking for President Washington. When he asked someone "Which gentleman was President-General Washington?" the man responded, "The one on his knees leading prayer!" President Lincoln issued a proclamation of a day of "humiliation, fasting, and prayer" in 1863. It was President Franklin Roosevelt who called for our nation to unite in prayer as American troops stormed the beaches of Normandy in WWII... and just 7 ½ years ago it was President G.W. Bush who asked our nation to unite in prayer after the September 11th attacks on our country! I remember thereafter, seeing signs in public school yards, government buildings, yards of homes, on automobiles, and church yards saying, "God Bless the U.S.A." – and "Pray 4-our Nation!" WOW, how quickly we forget!

This nation was founded upon principles and values. The fathers of this nation were not perfect, but they did believe in God and it was their faith that made the U.S.A. the great nation that it is today. Many times they wrote and spoke about their faith. These men believed that you couldn't call yourself a Patriot if you didn't believe in God. They believed that the Bible should be taught in public schools along with a daily prayer. Over the past few decades, Christians have just stood back and allowed a minority take God out of our nation little by little. I have noticed that in our new society, it has even became unpopular to say that the U.S.A. is a great nation, and slowly we are removing the words "Under God." I believe that political correctness has softened and weakened our nation, and it's time to claim the U.S.A. back for the Kingdom of God!

On May 7, 2009, we as a nation will celebrate our 58th Annual Observance of The National Day of Prayer. As a local Pastor and a regional Chaplain, I join with other believers to unite in prayer for our nation!!! These are uncertain times we are living in, and the United States needs above all things for her people to come together before God and in the spirit of our forefathers, seek His wisdom and His blessings!!! I still believe the scripture that says God will heal our land! My prayer is this:

"Heavenly Father, we praise and exalt Your Name! God forgive us as a nation for the sins of the past. Renew our hope in You as the living God. Speak to our leaders that they might once again seek Your divine wisdom about making decisions for our nation. We pray that You will remove the immorality that has infected this country, and bring Your people back to their knees. We end this prayer with a statement that has been said many times; GOD BLESS AMERICA AGAIN!"

If my people, which are called by my name, shall humble themselves, and pray, and seek my face, and turn from their wicked ways; then will I hear from heaven, and will forgive their sin, and will heal their land.
2 Chronicles 7:14 (KJV)

MINISTRY

*C*hristian ministry is defined as an activity by Christians to spread or express their faith **under the leadership** of Apostolic oversight. I have often defined ministry as "an overflow of God's wisdom, knowledge, grace, and mercy in your own life, and sharing it with others." Many times I hear the statement in the religious sector "that he/she is a minister". Over the years, I have came to ask this question to that statement. "A minister of what?"

Recently, I have had conversations with Buddhist ministers, Wicca Ministers, Occult Ministers, and "so called" Christian faith ministers. All of the above have some kind of credentials declaring them as ministers. But again I ask, "Ministers of what?" I tell the folks at Haven of Hope that I am a minister, not because I have an Rev. or Pastor in front of my name, but I am a minister because God has called me to minister and under Apostolic leadership, "I Minister – or share my overflow with others!"

About two years ago, a gentleman came to me introducing himself as a "Pastor." When I asked him where he was a Pastor he said, "No where…." Well, a shepherd is only a shepherd because he/she has sheep! A Pastor is only a Pastor if he/she has a flock! This is where proper **Apostolic Leadership** and **Oversight** comes in to play. You see, not everyone called to the ministry is called to preach or teach! The Bible says, "Some are called to be Apostles, some are called to be Prophets, and some are called Pastors, Evangelists, and Teachers…." I believe that all are called to do something, but all are not called to do the same thing! Some are called to Deacon; some are called to play music, and some are called to the arts. See my point? Without proper Apostolic leadership, we can be led astray and away from God's calling on our lives! I have seen many good folks walk away from God's calling on their lives to chase a dream of becoming a great music minister or a great Evangelist. Greatness can only be found in God's will for our life!!!

Let me end with some advice for those who believe they have a call to minister on their lives! Number one, find a Pastor – Apostle – Bishop for yourself! We all need spiritual accountability, and it's VERY prideful to think differently! Number two, get plugged into a local church! If you are truly "called to the ministry", then you will never need to make room for your ministry; your ministry will make room for itself!" (A quote from Pastor Bryan Lamm.) Number three, learn to serve. As a minister, serving God is serving others!!! Learn to serve the local church, serve your Pastor, and serve the community! Remember,

ALL ministries begin with the "Ministry of Helps!" Number four, learn that your number-one ministry is at home with your family (your spouse and kids). I have seen a lot of ministers soar in the ministry, but their own family goes straight to hell. If I can't pray with/minister to Benita and the girls, then I have no business ministering to others! And last, forget about the titles and prefixes! I was a Pastor several years before I became ordained and licensed. Having papers stating that I am ordained and licensed and/or having a degree in Divinity means nothing unless I'm walking in an overflow of the ministry in my own life and sharing that overflow with others!!!

I now take that overflow and shine like a light to a dark and dying world!

Matthew 5:16 KJV

[16]Let your light so shine before men, that they may see your good works, and glorify your Father which is in heaven.

Matthew 28:18-20 KJV

[18]And Jesus came and spake unto them, saying, All power is given unto me in heaven and in earth. [19]Go ye therefore, and teach all nations, baptizing them in the name of the Father, and of the Son, and of the Holy Ghost: [20]Teaching them to observe all things whatsoever I have commanded you: and, lo, I am with you always, even unto the end of the world. Amen.

MOTHERS

*T*he modern **Mother's Day** holiday was created by Anna Jarvis from Taylor County WV, as a day for each family to honor its mother. In 1912, she trademarked the phrases "second Sunday in May" and "Mother's Day", and created the Mother's Day International Association. The day is designed for each family to honor their mother before God. Ironically, it was about nine years after the first official Mother's Day, commercialization of the U.S. holiday became so rampant that Anna Jarvis herself became a major opponent of what the holiday had become and spent all her inheritance and the rest of her life fighting what she saw as an abuse of the celebration. Later, commercial and other exploitations of the use of Mother's Day infuriated Anna and she made her criticisms known throughout her time.

Anna Jarvis created Mother's Day to give special honor to our mothers, whom so deserve! When thinking about Mother's Day and looking at the Bible we can see that God commands us to give honor to our mothers;

12Honour thy father and thy mother: that thy days may be long upon the land which the LORD thy God giveth thee (Exodus 20:12 KJV).

In the New Testament Jesus, Himself honored His earthly mother with very high respect! We know that when a person is dying, it's the most important things in their lives that they dwell on. In the same light, it was on Jesus' cross, moments before He died, that he thought of His mother! And one of the seven phrases He said from the cross was addressing His Earthly Mother:

26When Jesus therefore saw his mother, and the disciple standing by, whom he loved, he saith unto his mother, Woman, behold thy son! 27Then saith he to the disciple, Behold thy mother! And from that hour that disciple took her unto his own home (John 19:26-27 KJV).

This Mother's Day Sunday I challenge you to obey God's Word and Do as Jesus did; Give Honor to Your Mother!!! I pray that God would Bless All of our Mothers this week and through the weekend in a special way! Amen.

This message was preached on Mother's Day 2009

APOSTOLIC
OVERSIGHT

*W*hat is Apostolic Oversight? No, this is not a title made up by contemporary Charismatic churches. The New Testament Church was founded upon Apostolic Oversight, with the foundation being the Apostles, and Jesus Christ serving as chief corner stone (Ephesians 2:20). Paul said, "I have laid the foundation, and another buildeth thereon" (1 Corinthians 3:10 KJV). Throughout the Old and New Testaments, God always uses man to serve as oversight to His people. Abraham, Isaac, and Jacob, Moses, Aaron, Joshua, Samuel, Elijah; the list from the Old Testament of God using men to give spiritual oversight goes on and on... And from the New Testament, if you think about it, Jesus Christ placed Himself in the hands of John the Baptist before performing one miracle. From Peter to Paul, the New Testament Church was set in motion by Apostolic Oversight. Paul identified himself as a preacher and an Apostle:

*1 Timothy 2:7 **KJV***
"I am ordained a preacher and an apostle…"

First let's set the record straight; Apostolic Oversight is not about what the Apostolic minister takes from the local church, but rather what the Apostolic Minister gives to the local church. Paul said to the church in Thessalonica that his coming to them "was not in vain" or "not empty-handed" (1 Thessalonians 2:1).

So, what is the purpose of Apostolic Oversight? First is spiritual counsel. The Apostle/Bishop can give Godly counsel to the local church, Pastor, co-Pastors, Associate Pastors, Elders, Deacons, and the Church Body. Next is to bring and maintain Biblical order in the local church. The Apostle/Bishop touches every ministry of the local hurch. As spiritual oversight, they give the congregation someone to appeal to if a Pastor or Elder falls into sin or strays away from the church doctrine. They can help restore the man/woman back to God's calling in their lives. I believe that a Pastor or Elder should never be removed without the counsel of Apostolic Oversight. The Apostle/ Bishop, gives the Pastor someone to be accountable to. They encourage and uplift the local Pastor as he/she encourages and uplifts the local church body. This helps keep the Pastors from "spiritual burn out." They literally serve as a Pastor to the Pastors. Everyone needs someone and the office of the Apostle/Bishop serves as that someone or a go to person for the local Pastor.

Apostolic Oversight is all about relationship. A while back a gentleman came to me and said that he felt the Lord leading him to me as a spiritual oversight. The only problem was that I did not feel the Lord leading me to him. If the Lord was really sending him to me, then I think that the Lord would have probably told me about it! When my spiritual covering came to me, I knew that it was God and so did he! It was God bringing us together, not man... Paul called himself a spiritual father to Timothy:

1 Timothy 1:2 *KJV*
"Unto Timothy, my own <u>son</u> in the <u>faith</u>: Grace, mercy, and peace, from God our Father and Jesus Christ our Lord."

A true Apostle/Bishop, serves as a spiritual father to the local Pastors as the local Pastors serve as a spiritual father to the local church body. It's God's order for His Church.

I could go on and talk about how the Bible teaches us not to walk alone and how we need each other. I believe that everyone is called to and needs a local church and a local Pastor! And I also believe that every local Pastor needs a spiritual covering or spiritual oversight – an Apostle/Bishop to help keep him/her in check and in God's order. The author of Hebrews calls followers who are not under spiritual authority "bastards or fatherless" (Hebrews 12:8), and calls all of us to be subject to "spiritual fathers:"

Hebrews 12:9 KJV
"Furthermore we have had fathers of our flesh which corrected us, and we gave them reverence: shall we

not much rather be in subjection unto the Father of spirits, and live?"

In today's culture, and even in the modern day church, it is unpopular to talk about spiritual accountability and personal responsibility. God has designed an order for His Church to function. Apostolic Oversight is God's order! Below is a pyramid of the New Testament Church. Notice that the Anointing and the vision of God's Church will always flow from the top down.

DIVIDED WE FALL - UNITED WE STAND

*A*s I read the New Testament and how the early church was formed, one word keeps jumping out at me - "Unity!!!" Jesus spent so much time trying to unite, bring together, and connect His Disciples one to another forming one Body or One Unit – The Church! Jesus warned His Disciples about division. In the Matthew 12:25 Jesus said, "Every kingdom divided against itself is brought to desolation; and every city or house divided against itself shall not stand" (KJV). That word desolation means; unhappiness, misery, despair, sadness, and depression. Think about it, division births all of these negative afflictions. We've heard of the fruits of the Spirit, but it's like these are the rotten fruits of the evil spirit of division.

We can look at the postmodern world that we live in; we can see the Church divided against herself! I used to pray that the Pentecostals would learn to fellowship with their Baptist brothers and sisters, but now I would just love to see the Pentecostals learn to get along with other Pentecostals, let alone other denominations! In our culture, we have so many churches forming for the simple fact that Christian folks just can't get along. What will we do if we get the Heaven? Despite popular opinion, Heaven will not be sectioned off! No, there will not be a Pentecostal Heaven, a Baptist Heaven, a Catholic Heaven, a Methodist Heaven, etc.... There will only be ONE Heaven, and we will all be together in one place, worshiping God for eternity with one voice! The denominational name tags we wear so proudly here on earth will do us no good on the other side, regardless where you go! Think about it, if you go down, the denominational name tags will burn off. And if you go up, the denominational name tags will fall off!

I believe we are living in desperate times! These are times of great opportunity for the local church, every denomination, to come together on common ground. "That God is God, and He is the Only Living God; Jesus is His Son who died for our sins. Through Jesus we can be saved, and through Jesus we can receive God's power through His Holy Spirit!" Can we put our worship styles and church doctrines aside for a while, and seek God's glory and salvation for our nation? Jesus Prayed in John 17:11, "that they may be one, as we are" (KJV).

A few years ago I was invited to participate in a county wide revival. Of course I agreed very quickly. We were having a strategic planning meeting about a week outside the meetings when a lady stood up and said, "The local Baptist church isn't participating in our meetings, so we will just show them how to have

revival and they can just sit on their pews and watch."
WOW! When she was done venting about the Baptist,
I stood up, grabbed my Bible and planner and started
to walk out. One of the Pastors asked me what was
wrong and I answered, "This is not God's will or His
way, if we are having special services just to show
the Baptist how to have church then I do not want to
be a part of it!" The local Pastor that seemed to be in
charge assured me that this was not the focus of these
meetings. I foolishly believed him. Without getting
into too many details, I was asked to open up and
preach the first night. The meetings started off "on
fire" with over one hundred folks gathering together.
Folks even came out of the local bars to hear what
was going on. After I was done preaching, the folks
from the bars stood up and applauded with the other
folks there. What a sight, Christians from all different
backgrounds praying, singing, and worshiping
together!

I wish I could end this on a positive note, but
throughout the week pride and jealousy set in and
the rest is history. The last night about twelve folks
came out to end this so called "Revival!" I remember
thinking "why can't we just put our differences aside
and have church?" I believe God was probably
thinking the same thing.

Time and time again I have seen God's children try
to come together, but it seems like each time pride
moves in and stops God's will. So I ask this, "Can it
be done?" the answer is, "YES IT CAN!" God has
used me to bring His Word to so many different
denominations. A local Nazarene church had asked
my wife and I to speak two nights at their revival. As

I stood in this traditional Nazarene church and preached, the fire of God fell in a mighty way. I looked into the congregation – half Nazarene and half from my church. You couldn't tell who was who. They were all worshiping as children of God! The local Pastor had no pride and he received the Word along with his people. I gave an altar call and many came forward and the Nazarene Pastor and I prayed for the folks side by side! Even though we worship differently, we both are ministers of the Most High and we were able to put down our differences for that night and have CHURCH!

Here is another testimony of how God can bring unity to His people. We had Mike Warnke preaching a revival at our church. A Pastor from a church in a neighboring town, in the same county as my church, closed his doors for their regular Wednesday night church service and brought his congregation over to our church to join our revival service! What a testimony of God's heart for His Church! The two churches had such a great time together worshiping God and praying one for another.

I end this column with a challenge to Pastors: take this Brother's lead and let's join together in Christ and watch God's Revival Fire ignite our nation! Remember the old proverb, **"Divided We Fall/ United We Stand!"** Let's Stand for God's Word together and see God heal our land!

After I wrote this blog and posted it on the church's website, I received a couple of Christian Hate letters from preachers. Let me share some of things that they wrote. One "Pastor" wrote me a letter stating that I should be careful letting men who have been divorced and/or have had past affairs participate in church events. WOW! What a great example of a judgmental Pharisee! If God forgives all of our sins, and all of our past, then why make folks wear a scarlet "A" around their neck for the rest of their lives? To that "Pastor", I say, "Come on, lets get off our holier than thou platform, and he without sin can cast the first stone!" I believe in forgiveness and restoration in God's Kingdom, for everyone.

I received another letter from a "minister" in NY saying that God does not want unity in between the churches, and basically that all of the other churches are wrong except his! To him and other judgmental preachers, I say that hell will be full of prideful so called "Reverends" who thought they were it! Having a "Rev." in front of your name does nothing for me; it's your lifestyle that defines who you are not your title. It's your relationship with Jesus that defines your eternity!

Despite these few people who are way off, I still believe that God is birthing a great revival with the local church – His Church!

XV

A STORY OF ONE MAN - 2 KINGS

*T*oday's message is a story of two Kings. The first King was born to earth as a son of a carpenter named Joseph from a virgin named Mary. He was raised from what would have been at the bottom of the social ladder; just an average family. Then 33 years later, this son of a carpenter who had now become a preacher, rode into Jerusalem on a donkey, fulfilling prophecy from the Old Testament. Picture the city filled with thousands of people ready to celebrate the Jewish Passover; when God sent a deliverer to His people to free them from captivity. Those with the blood on their doors escaped death! The Passover was literally a celebration of LIFE!!!

Now on this day, this son of a carpenter who became a prophet and preacher came into town. Who was this Jesus? He was baptized in water by a radical preacher named John the Baptist, after 3 years of preaching the Good News of God's Kingdom. It was 3 years of going to city to city, healing the sick, making the lame walk, the blind see, the mute speak, and the dead rise! Three years of forgiving sins and setting captives free from evil spirits. Three years of confronting religion and telling the Pharisees that they were hypocrites...Now this Jesus was riding into the city on a donkey.

LUKE 19:35-40 KJV

35And they brought him (the donkey) to Jesus: and they cast their garments upon the colt, and they set Jesus thereon. 36And as he went, they spread their clothes in the way. 37And when he was come nigh, even now at the descent of the Mount of Olives, the whole multitude of the disciples began to rejoice and praise God with a loud voice for all the mighty works that they had seen; 38Saying, Blessed be the King that cometh in the name of the Lord: peace in heaven, and glory in the highest. 39And some of the Pharisees from among the multitude said unto him, Master, rebuke thy disciples. 40And he answered and said unto them, I tell you that, if these should hold their peace, the stones would immediately cry out.

As Jesus rode into the city, the Bible says a multitude, a massive amount, a very large crowd, or the whole host came out to greet Him! Watch this, the whole host, or the whole city came out to welcome Jesus into the city as a KING!!! In verse 38 they said, "Blessed be the King." Notice they worshiped Him as KING with a LOUD VOICE! When the religious leaders said quiet them down, Jesus responded "IF they don't worship me the ROCKS will...." I have said many times that when religion tries to quiet down your worship, when religion tries to steal your praise, when religion tries to contain you worshiping YOUR KING, DO what Jesus did... Say, "Devil you might steal a lot from me, but know this -- YOU CAN

NEVER HAVE MY KING'S WORSHIP!!! That belongs to, and will always belong, to JESUS!!!"

Now we see that Jesus' earthly Kingship was short-lived. The same multitude that worshiped Him on Palm Sunday was the same multitude who cried,"Crucify Him!" on Good Friday! What a difference five days make!!! I've said many times that I cringe when people stand up and loudly say "I'm with you man...." I tell Benita, "In five days they will be crucifying me." Time and time again folks have stood up and said, "I am with you and the vision that God is leading you in," and in a matter of weeks they drift away! Watch the folks that are so vocal about their allegiance; most of the time it's the quiet folks that are praying and standing with and for you. Get this from today's text, "In God's Kingdom there is NO ROOM for Christian Flip Floppers!!! God is looking for a people who are SOLD OUT to Him and sold out to the vision that God has placed in them!!!

The title is 1-Man/2-Kings right? Well, here comes the second King. You see, the Jews were looking for a triumphant earthly king to ride into the city on a big horse with full armor, kill the Roman army and raise them up. But Jesus was humble and seemed to accept and forgive everyone -- even the Romans, the Greeks, the Samaritans, the prostitutes, the adulterers, the fornicators, and thieves. Really, the only group of people that Jesus was not received by was the religious leaders. The first KING who rode into the city on PALM SUNDAY was the Lamb ready to be sacrificed for our sins... but that Lamb has risen into a NEW KING!!! Now let's look at the second King.

Revelation 1:13-18 KJV

[10] I was in the Spirit on the Lord's day, and heard behind me a great voice, as of a trumpet, [11] Saying, I am Alpha and Omega, the first and the last...

[13] And in the midst of the seven candlesticks one like unto the Son of man, clothed with a garment down to the foot, and girt about the paps with a golden girdle. [14] His head and his hairs were white like wool, as white as snow; and his eyes were as a flame of fire; [15] And his feet like unto fine brass, as if they burned in a furnace; and his voice as the sound of many waters. [16] And he had in his right hand seven stars: and out of his mouth went a sharp twoedged sword: and his countenance was as the sun shineth in his strength. [17] And when I saw him, I fell at his feet as dead. And he laid his right hand upon me, saying unto me, Fear not; I am the first and the last: [18] I am he that liveth, and was dead; and, behold, I am alive for evermore, Amen; and have the keys of hell and of death.

And there's more...

Revelation 19:11-16 KJV

[11] And I saw heaven opened, and behold a white horse; and he that sat upon him was called Faithful and True, and in righteousness he doth judge and make war. [12] His eyes were as a flame of fire, and on his head were many crowns; and he had a name written, that no man knew, but he himself. [13] And he was clothed with a vesture dipped in blood: and his name is called The Word of God. [14] And the armies which were in heaven followed him upon white horses, clothed in fine linen, white and clean. [15] And out of his mouth goeth a sharp sword, that with it he should smite the nations: and he shall rule them with a rod of iron: and he treadeth the winepress of the fierceness

and wrath of Almighty God. *16And he hath on his vesture and on his thigh a name written, KING OF KINGS, AND LORD OF LORDS.*

And there's more...

Revelation 21:1-7 KJV

1And I saw a new heaven and a new earth: for the first heaven and the first earth were passed away; and there was no more sea. 2And I John saw the holy city, new Jerusalem, coming down from God out of heaven, prepared as a bride adorned for her husband. 3And I heard a great voice out of heaven saying, Behold, the tabernacle of God is with men, and he will dwell with them, and they shall be his people, and God himself shall be with them, and be their God. 4And God shall wipe away all tears from their eyes; and there shall be no more death, neither sorrow, nor crying, neither shall there be any more pain: for the former things are passed away. 5And he that sat upon the throne said, Behold, I make all things new. And he said unto me, Write: for these words are true and faithful. 6And he said unto me, It is done. I am Alpha and Omega, the beginning and the end. I will give unto him the fountain of the water of life freely. 7He that overcometh shall inherit all things; and I will be his God, and he shall be my son.

One man/two kings; King of the Jews who became the KING of HEAVEN! Jesus was the slain Lamb, but NOW He's the Risen Savior! Jesus was the King of the Jews, but NOW He's the KING OF KINGS!!! Jesus once carried His cross, but NOW He carries a scepter. Jesus once wore a crown of thorns, but He NOW wears a Crown of Glory! Jesus was called a false prophet, but NOW He's called Faithful and True.

Jesus did ride an ass or a donkey, but NOW He rides a White Horse. (One time I was preaching this and said, "Jesus got off His ass now its time for the church to get off theirs!") Jesus was once worshiped on earth as king, but NOW and forevermore He will be praised as the KING of Kings and LORD of Lords! Amen!

XV

HE DIDN'T LIKE PREACHERS

*T*his story is about a personal experience I had ministering with a gentleman that was dying of cancer; this visit literally changed my life.

I was about to visit this gentleman as a Chaplain. Everyone, including the man's wife, told me how he wasn't religious and didn't like preachers. I explained to the man's family that I was not there to promote my spiritual beliefs or my church, and that my role was to provide spiritual support to him. Never the less, they wished me luck with a snicker as I entered the patient's bedroom. He was an elderly man, a retired coal miner with large rough hands and a raspy voice. As I entered the room, he looked up at me about as mean as a man could look and he said, "Who are you and what do you want?" I smiled and told him that "I was a son of a coal miner and I was there to hear some good mining stories." He sat right up in his bed and spent the next two hours telling me life-changing stories about the coal mines and life in the "old days."

He told me about the great depression and how life was back then. Then he began to tell me about his life and different stories about his childhood and his family. He talked with me for about two hours; he laughed as the stories kept unfolding. I sat beside him and listened to the all of the tales about a time gone by.

When his tales were finished, he asked me how I made my living. I told him that I was a preacher and a Chaplain. Then the next words from his mouth completely shocked me. He said in a deep rough voice, "Well aren't you going to read that book (pointing to my Bible) to me?" I smiled and asked him what scripture was his favorite. He said that he thought they all were good, and I could read whatever I wanted. So, I opened my Bible to the Gospel of John 3:3 and read it to him.

John3:3 (KJV)
3Jesus answered and said unto him, Verily, verily, I say unto thee, Except a man be born again, he cannot see the kingdom of God.

After I read the scripture and explained to him what born again meant, and how no one can go to Heaven without Jesus; I asked him if I could pray with him. He swallowed as he nodded, so I reached for his hand and prayed a blessing over him and his family. I then asked him if he would like to pray the sinner's prayer. He nodded again, and we prayed a short sinner's prayer together. After I ended my prayer with amen, this hard shell man, who "hated preachers", started to cry a river of tears as he began to pray and praise God aloud. He lifted his hands and shouted "Praise

God! Praise the Lord!" His wife, now standing at the door with her eyes red and flowing with tears, came in and embraced her newly saved husband. The three of us cried and praised God together for about thirty minutes. I joined hands with the both of them and prayed a blessing over them and went on my way.

Throughout the next few months, I was able to visit with him and his wife on several different occasions. Each time we read scriptures, prayed, and praised God together. After he passed away, his family told me how my visits changed his life. But the real truth is that the **visits changed my life.**

Sometimes I still stand in awe in how God uses me to touch lives. I count it a privilege and honor to serve folks, throughout the region, in their final days here on earth. When I became a Hospice Chaplain, everyone kept telling me about how sad the job would be and how depressed I would become. It's the opposite; I count it a joy to minister in the homes of strangers. I rejoice in the fact that God uses me to help walk so many of His children home to eternity! There is nothing sad about watching a saint close his/her eyes here on earth and watch angels escort them into Heaven…

Luke 16:22
"And it came to pass, that the beggar died, and was carried by the angels into Abraham's bosom:"

Many times people ask me about where healing comes in when praying for all of the terminally ill patients. I believe in healing, and if God chooses to heal them here on earth, that's great. But I believe that Heaven is a place of total healing! Heaven is our reward! Sometimes we try to keep our loved ones here with us when the Lord is calling them home to be with Him! It's tough to let go, but when they have fought the good fight and their time has come to an end, we should rejoice in celebration of their life and their reward in Heaven. Heaven is a place with no suffering, no afflictions, no pain, no confusion, and no worry or stress! When I get to Heaven, I'll be met with an entourage of believers who have gone before me and join them in an eternity of celebration!!! Amen!

Revelation 21:4 (KJV)

"And God shall wipe away all tears from their eyes; and there shall be no more death, neither sorrow, nor crying, neither shall there be any more pain: for the former things are passed away."

Revelation 14:13 (KJV)

"And I heard a voice from heaven saying unto me, Write, Blessed are the dead which die in the Lord from henceforth: Yea, saith the Spirit, that they may rest from their labours; and their works do follow them."

THE LOVE OF HER LIFE

*T*he love of her life, he had been fighting cancer for the past two years, had just been released from curative care and the world as she knew it was quickly crashing down. He had lived a good life, working six to seven days per week and raising their three children. He had become the greatest grandfather that a man could ever be! He had received God into his life about three years prior. He lived his life for work, but when God saved him he changed from night to day. He became one of the greatest men of God that I have ever met. He served others and served his church with all of his strength. But now the time had come for him to decide about his quality of life. He never wanted to live like this – not being able to swallow solid food, drink straight water (without thickener), and be in severe pain every day. There were no alternatives available to pursue to prolong his life short of a miracle.

With hope fading away, she called me and asked what she should do now? I asked her if she knew about

Hospice. "Well, not exactly," she answered, so I explained. "Hospice Care is an organization that helps people who are very sick, like your husband, to be cared for at home." She didn't say anything else at the time, and I didn't press the issue. However, that afternoon she called me back and said quite out of the blue, "Hospice is for people who are seriously ill and want to be comfortable." "Yes, you are right," I said. "Can you make the call for me?" So, I called Hospice for her.

Thankfully, the caring, capable, and committed staff of Hospice was able to be there for them. Over the next year the nurses, nursing assistant, Chaplain, and social worker offered their "Helping Hands and Caring Hearts" in all that needed to be done. The Hospice Care nurses sat with the family through the last couple days and when the time came for "the love of her life" to take the step into eternity, the caring hearts of Hospice stayed by her side walking her through the healing process. Over the next 13-months the Grief and Bereavement Counselor met with her weekly, holding her hand, praying with her, and helping her broken heart heal.

Today, three years after losing the love of her life, she has opened up her home to other people who have experienced the loss of a loved one. She hosts a weekly Grief Support meeting with Hospice, and through helping others she has found inner peace and healing herself. She has become so strong, standing on God's Word for her life. I see her often at the altar at church praying for others, holding their hands and walking them through the same healing process that she had gone through. While losing a loved one to a serious illness can never be easy, I have come to see the value of active participation in care-giving to Hospice patients by their family and friends. While this may seem odd, I have heard the lady in the featured story saying to others that "my husband had a good death." By that she means he was able to die as he wished, at home in his own bed, surrounded by the people he loved the most listening to his favorite worship music.

Along with serving as a Pastor at my church, I count it an honor in serving as a Hospice Chaplain! There are so many stories to tell about how God has used me as a Chaplain to bring peace into the most chaotic circumstances. I pray that He would continue to use me according to His will.

THAT'S ONE GREAT DAD!

*A*s a man, I'm convinced that we "men" are commonly misunderstood by women. Men, the women in our lives may not always be able to understand our conversations or know just what were thinking, but they can see and understand our actions. I believe that it is a basic truth that our actions speak louder than our words! As dads and husbands, it's our actions that become our language of love to our families. In this chapter, I want us to see the actions of a father in the Bible that demonstrated his love for his family in a mighty way. His name was Jairus.

In the book of Luke 8:40-42, we meet Jairus as he came to see Jesus. Jairus' twelve year old daughter was dying, and he had no where to turn and no hope, until he came to Jesus.

Luke 8:40-42 GWT
40 When Jesus came back, a crowd welcomed him. Everyone was expecting him. 41 A man named Jairus,

175

a synagogue leader, arrived and quickly bowed down in front of Jesus. He begged Jesus to come to his home. 42 His only daughter, who was about twelve years old, was dying. As Jesus went, the people were crowding around him.

I love this story for several reasons. Number one, Jairus was a leader in the synagogue; he worked with the same folks that were plotting to kill Jesus. But when he received the news that his daughter wasn't going to make it, he left the judgmental "better than thou" folks and pressed through the crowd to fall at Jesus' feet! This dad didn't care what people thought, he didn't care if he lost his job, he knew his mission was to find Jesus then bring Jesus to his house to heal his family! This is truly ONE GREAT DAD!

I believe that our mission as dads is to be like Jairus. As fathers, we can do a lot of things for our families - earn lots of money, buy lots of things, take trips to places, go shopping, play sports, go hunting or fishing; the list goes on and on. All of these things are fine and somewhat important, but I believe that our **most important** task as a dad, above all other things, is to follow Jairus' lead - go get Jesus and bring Him to our families!

If you continue to read the text, you'll see that Jairus received news, as he and Jesus were walking to his house, that his daughter had died. But Jairus knew that he was walking with Jesus and ignored the news and kept walking. He could have received the news and become bitter. He could have said Jesus you didn't come quickly enough. But he didn't do any of that; he just ignored the report of man and kept walking home with Jesus. I believe that when you're walking with Jesus, and you're in His perfect will, bad news just won't hold you back! Jairus just kept walking with Jesus; what a mighty testimony of One Great Dad!

Let me end this story by telling you that Jesus did raise Jairus' daughter from the dead. Jairus' perseverance, dedication, devotion, and commitment to his family paid off! In today's world, I know that several dads reading this may be going through some very bad and uncertain circumstances. I pray that you would take the position that God designed for you, as the father of your house, and go to Jesus, fall on your knees, and receive His help! Like this dad named Jairus, you too will see God raise your family up and you'll become "One Great Dad!" Remember your miracle may just be a prayer away!

Here are some basic points from the story in our text. First, Jairus knew that his daughter and his family were much more important than his job at the synagogue. Men, we need to prioritize our lives. Work is important, but work should never become our life! I have prayed with hundreds of folks that only had weeks to live and never have any of them told me that they wish they would have worked more hours or bought more stuff. Our family is a gift from God; we need to take time out from our busy weeks and spend time with the wife and our children! Our real job is to be there for our family. Our real job is to be a DAD to our sons and daughters!!! I believe that when the men of our nation begin to step up to the plate and become DADS that we will see the morality in this country turn around!

Next, we see that Jairus laid down his manly pride and fell at Jesus' feet. Pride holds us back so often from receiving our miracles. We also see that when Jairus didn't get his miracle in the form that he thought, he still kept walking with Jesus. Sometimes we must be willing to walk that extra mile with the Lord, even when things aren't happening the way that we thought they should. I remember when my Kaitie was dying. Every time we would expect God to heal her, she would get sicker. I remember telling God that if He wanted to take her home, that I would still serve Him and worship Him, regardless! Looking back, it was shortly after that prayer that we received our miracle and Kaitie was healed! Like Jairus, we didn't receive the report of man but we received Gods report and kept walking with Jesus!

I read all of the statistics about fathers in this country. But I still believe that God is on the throne and He is going to raise up young men to take their place as fathers to their children again. I believe that the family structure in this nation that has fallen over the years is going to be restored, as the men of the nation turn away from worldly ways to God – fall at the feet of Jesus – and allow the Holy Spirit to guide their steps! Amen.

THE EARTH IS
THE LORD'S?

*A*s I was watching the news the other day I began to focus on all of the bad things happening around the globe. All of the violence and unhappiness that's plaguing the airways can really get you thinking and doing some soul searching. I begin to ask myself questions like, why is God allowing so much bad to happen? And why is all of this bad stuff happening to good people? In the small town that I Pastor in, the local police just uncovered a serial killer who may have murdered at least five women. One body was buried just down the road a few miles from where I live, and one of the victims lived in my town and was friends with several of my church members. WOW. Things like this may happen on TV, but never in a small town like Philippi, WV. Well, the truth is that bad things happen everywhere. But why? I read in the 24th Psalm that the earth belongs to the Lord. If the earth is the Lord's, then why doesn't He do something about all of this evil in His world?

Psalm 24 GWT

1 The earth and everything it contains is the LORD's. The world and all who live in it are his. 2 He laid its foundation on the seas and set it firmly on the rivers. 3 Who may go up the LORD's mountain? Who may stand in his holy place? 4 The one who has clean hands and a pure heart and does not long for what is false or lie when he is under oath. 5 This person will receive a blessing from the LORD and righteousness from God, his savior. 6 This is the person, who seeks him, who searches for the face of the God of Jacob. 7 Lift your heads, you gates. Be lifted, you ancient doors, so that the king of glory may come in. 8 Who is this king of glory? The LORD, strong and mighty! The LORD, heroic in battle! 9 Lift your heads, you gates. Be lifted, you ancient doors, so that the king of glory may come in. 10 Who, then, is this king of glory? The LORD of Armies is the king of glory!

We read that David wrote that the earth and all that is in it belong to the Lord right? So, I ask this question to you - is the earth truly the Lord's? Is the United States of America truly the Lord's? For decades now, our government has given God an eviction notice and asked Him to leave our nation! The earth and everything it contains is the LORD's. The world and all who live in it are His? Well, not the U.S.A.! A few years ago a group of Christians were preaching in Clarksburg on the street during the Italian Heritage Festival. The police came up and told them that they had to leave because they were disturbing the peace. At a festival with alcohol, loud music, a carnival... well, you get the picture. But a church group preaching is disturbing the peace. The earth is the

Lord's? Not in Clarksburg, WV during the Italian Heritage Festival. A while back, a Christian girl ran for class president at my town's local high school and gave her testimony during her speech. She got in trouble and as a result all public speeches were banned at that school. In the U.S., prayer to God seems to be forbidden at our schools. Several times, Muslim kids are given the freedom to pray during school, but Christian kids are shunned. The Bible is censored, but some schools use the Koran as a teaching tool for social studies in studying the Middle East! I read about a school in California that had a Muslim Day during school hours where the kids dressed up like Muslims and studied their faith. Could you imagine the outcry if we were to have a Christian Day during school time at a public school? The earth is the Lord's? Not in our public school systems. In Bridgeport, WV, a picture of Jesus hung for years, but one man said he didn't like it and our supreme court took Jesus down! The earth is the Lord's? Not at Bridgeport High School.

If the earth and everything it contains is the Lord's, the world and all who live in it are His. Then why is He allowing these "politically correct" pencil necks to push Him out IF it belongs to him? I believe we can find the answer in Genesis 1:26 (ASV).

"And God said, Let us make man in our image, after our likeness: and let them have dominion over the fish of the sea, and over the birds of the heavens, and over the cattle, and over all the earth, and over every creeping thing that creepeth upon the earth."

The word dominion means *power, authority, and control*. The earth and everything it contains is the Lord's, but He has given the control or dominion to us!!! God gave Adam dominion over the earth. Adam gave the dominion to the devil, and Jesus came to take the dominion away from the devil. Jesus then gave the dominion back to us! So we now have dominion over the earth.

So, why is there so much bad in the world? We can't blame God; we can't even blame the devil. His power was stripped by Jesus! We need to look in the mirror and blame ourselves. If the dominion, power, authority, and control of the earth belong to us, then it is up to us to exercise the power that God has given us and change the world. How do we do that? One person at a time, starting with ourselves!

TAMMY FAYE

*T*oday's topic is a bit different than some of the other topics I have addressed in the past. Most of us have heard the name Tammy Faye (Baker) Messner. Tamara "Tammy" Faye Messner was an American Christian singer, evangelist, entrepreneur, author, talk show host, and television personality. She was the former wife of televangelist, and later convicted felon, Jim Baker, and she co-hosted with him on *The PTL Club*. Tammy Faye was famous for her heavy makeup, thick mascara and false eyelashes.

Tammy Faye became the butt end of jokes for several years with stand up comics, and I'm sorry to say several preachers and Christians. It is easy to judge and condemn Tammy Faye for her past, but I read in the Bible that God forgives our past! The only person who had a right to judge was Jesus, and He chose not to. I find Tammy Faye and her story fascinating on so many levels. I never watched *PTL,* so I have very few memories of her on Christian broadcasting. My memory of her is a lady in the spotlight sharing the good news of God's kingdom and His forgiveness, and taking personal criticisms on the chin with a smile.

Tammy Faye's 11-year battle with cancer was highly publicized, as she made several appearances on different talk shows. She was first diagnosed in March of 1996 with colon cancer, and the disease went into remission by the end of that year. Two weeks after her 62nd birthday in 2004, Tammy Faye made an appearance on *Larry King Live* and announced that she had inoperable lung cancer and was beginning chemotherapy. In November 2004, back on *Larry King Live*, she announced that she was cancer free once again. But on his program again on July 20, 2005 she announced that her cancer had returned. In October 2006, it was revealed that Tammy Faye had been admitted to a local Hospice program.

Tammy Faye was a guest by phone on Larry King Live on December 15, 2006 and stated that she was receiving Hospice care in her home. She talked about how great the Hospice program was and all of the great things that the Hospice staff had done to help make what would become her final year of life so peaceful. On July 19, 2007 she was again the interview subject on CNN's Larry King Live, where she said she weighed 65 pounds and was unable to eat solid food. She once again talked about the great care that she received from the local Hospice program. She talked about how good God is and how we should never judge others. She spoke about the joy of the Lord and His eternal forgiveness.

The very next day Tammy Faye (Baker) Messner passed away peacefully in her own home with her loved ones at her side. I started to think about how God had restored her faith, and how strong this lady's spirit was, even when her flesh was so weak. People can say this or that about Tammy Faye, but I believe that we serve a God full of grace and mercy. God is a God of forgiveness, and through Tammy Faye's testimony, I believe God forgave her of anything that she may have done in her past and restored the joy of her salvation. David in the Bible asked God to restore the joy of his salvation after he had fallen. And God did! If God did it for David, then he would do it for Tammy Faye, and He will do it for you and me too! There is no limit to God's grace, God's mercy, and God's forgiveness!!!

Let me end this story with a quote from Tammy Faye less than 24-hours before she died. "Don't let fear rule your life, live one day at a time, and never be afraid." Sounds like good advice to me. Thanks for the years of joy Tammy Faye. See ya' on the other side.

Follow The Yellow Brick Road?

*T*his is a message I preached a while ago; it was a very fun message to preach because it referenced one of my favorite movies, the Wizard of Oz.

Luke 15:11-19   NKJV

[11] Then He said: "A certain man had two sons. [12] And the younger of them said to his father, 'Father, give me the portion of goods that falls to me.' So he divided to them his livelihood. [13] And not many days after, the younger son gathered all together, journeyed to a far country, and there wasted his possessions with prodigal living. [14] But when he had spent all, there arose a severe famine in that land, and he began to be in want. [15] Then he went and joined himself to a citizen of that country, and he sent him into his fields to feed swine. [16] And he would gladly have filled his stomach with the pods that the swine ate, and no one gave him anything. [17] "But when he came to himself, he said, 'How many of my father's hired servants have bread enough and to spare, and I perish with hunger!

¹⁸ I will arise and go to my father, and will say to him, "Father, I have sinned against heaven and before you, ¹⁹ and I am no longer worthy to be called your son. Make me like one of your hired servants."'

In our text, the son made a decision to follow his dreams rather than to stay at the Father's house. Then he realized that things on the other side weren't the bed of roses that he thought... And he came to his senses when he was eating with the hogs. Sometimes I wonder how low God will need to let us go before we wake up. As I was reading this text and meditating about things happening around us, I began to think about a movie I loved as a kid, ***The Wizard of Oz.***

The Wizard of Oz is a children's novel published in 1900, and in 1902 it became a stage play. In 1939 it became an extremely popular, highly acclaimed film with Judy Garland as Dorothy. Dorothy was a young girl from Kansas who dreamed of a better place "somewhere over the rainbow." Most folks don't realize the rest of the story behind the book/movie, The Wizard of Oz. You see, the U.S. economy was very shaky at the time the book was written, and a decade before the movie was produced our stock market completely fell! The Wizard of Oz was written to resemble a people in a nation that the government had let down. Business industry had failed, and morality was sinking to an all time low! WOW! Does this sound ever so familiar? The Wizard of Oz has so many analogies throughout it. Oz itself represents a quest for money and earthly possessions! Oz is the abbreviation for the measuring of precious metals like gold and silver: ounces or OZ. A story about a quest for money and earthly possessions after the government has failed. Sounds like the U.S.A. in 2009!

Today were going to look at a different twist of this movie. Let's get into the story: Dorothy became dissatisfied with where she was and began to overlook all of the blessings she had. She had an Uncle Henry, Aunt Em, a little dog, Toto, and 3 wonderful friends who helped on the farm, and ALL WHO LOVED HER VERY MUCH!!! But rather than looking at what God gave her and thanking Him for all of her blessings, she went looking for new treasures "somewhere over the rainbow." Now let me say there is nothing wrong with having dreams, but Dorothy represents the kind of Christian who always has their head in the clouds. They never take the time to look around at the blessings God gives them, but always look for the next big thing, the next big movement of God. They are never willing to help out and serve where God has them, but are always chasing titles, talents, money, and power — always looking over the rainbow! These folks say the grass is greener at this church or that church, and then they get there and realize they are in more problems than before. If Dorothy knew what was over the rainbow, she never would have sang that stupid song!! She was over the rainbow – looking for her pot of gold. Well instead of finding her pot of gold, she found flying monkeys and witches trying to kill you!!!!

Watch this. When the storm came, everyone found shelter but Dorothy!!! Her head wasn't in looking for shelter, she was chasing rainbows. You need to know that when you're grounded in the Word - when the storms of life come, you can find shelter in Jesus.

Other folks may be flying all around, spinning around in their houses and running from witches flying by, but when you're grounded in the Word you find rest and shelter in His arms of Love!!!

In the story Dorothy ends up somewhere — over the rainbow stirring up the witches in the LAND! The only help she can find is following the advice of little people and a self-proclaimed witch! Well, she was a good witch right? I was ministering to a witch (follower of Wicca) a while back. He informed me that he was a white witch or a good witch. Let me caution you that a witch is a witch! If it isn't of God, then it's of the devil! Jesus said that He was the only way to the Father! God will not share His throne with a witch. Most folks enter into false teaching searching for truth. I have found that when you are not grounded in God's Word, then you will follow anyone and everyone, looking for a way out. How many times have we gotten sucked into sin just looking for a way out? Sin will take you farther than you wanted to go, cost you more than you wanted to pay, and keep you longer than you wanted to stay!!! In our story, Dorothy is now running from one witch and following the advice of another witch!

What's the advice? Follow the yellow brick road… follow gold – follow money – follow the world - but where will it lead you? To an earthly kingdom built on lies, misconceptions and shallow dreams! So let's get back to Dorothy. As she is walking down the yellow brick road, there comes an intersection. What way to go? Well, she doesn't know and the dog isn't talking, so she talks to a scarecrow without a brain! She was following a witch and munchkins, now she is following a brainless scarecrow! What an example of folks who leave the place God had called them to. They seem to follow anyone who will give them the time of day just to get some answers!

She found that the Scarecrow was worse off than she was. So here is Dorothy looking for her way back home, and now ON THE WAY she is helping the Scarecrow find his brain. So the two of them are "on the way" to find their miracle. Have you ever noticed that some of God's greatest miracles occur when you're "ON THE WAY?" Jesus is on the way to raise Jairus' daughter, and "ON THE WAY" He heals the woman with the issue of blood.

The Scarecrow represents agriculture straw or wheat - or the harvest!!! Church, the harvest is out there and confused – just hanging around waiting for someone to come along "ON THE WAY." The Scarecrow had a conflict in his head; the devil will attack the head first! It's in the mind that most spiritual warfare takes place! If you can learn to conquer the mind and your thoughts, then you'll go far in the Kingdom!

So Dorothy, and her new friend Scarecrow, are walking the yellow brick road. Next they find a Tin Woodsman; he represents a man who needs to be healed. His physical body can't move. The Tin Man was stuck in the same place for years and he can't move. Why? HE CAN'T REACH THE OIL!!! He tells Dorothy, just put some oil on me. This is a picture of today's church. Stuck in the same place for years, unable to dance, speak, and move. He had an ax, but couldn't use it! Today's church has the Word of God but can't use it due to a lack of oil! In the Bible, oil represents the Holy Spirit and the anointing from God! A storm came and he didn't have shelter or his oil. Does this sound familiar? We need to pray that God pours His Oil on our mouth so we might speak His Word and praise His Name. And on our hands and legs so we might clap and dance for His Joy.

Then the Tin Woodsman reveals that he needs a heart; he's empty on the inside. The surface issues were physical, but the real issue was in the heart! Remember, he represents the church. I believe that the church is facing heart issues. The church is so focused on man's opinion and church doctrine that it's lost her heart; the heart of God! God's heart for the local church is the heart to serve, the heart to save, the heart to forgive, and the heart to worship. Today's church needs a heart transplant!

Last, as the three are walking through the woods trying to avoid lions, and tigers, and bears (Oh my!), they meet a lion with a roar but no courage. Fear has overtaken him; he had lost his roar! He knew he was called to be the king of the jungle, but he had no ROAR!!! We have in us the Lion of Judah! I believe that God has placed a spiritual roar inside of us and when we release it demons tremble!!! God has told me that He is about ready to release FEAR from His people and release a ROAR, not from the king of the jungle, but from the King of Kings!!! If your born again, then you're a spiritual lion. Release the roar of the Lion of Judah!!!

Okay. They get to the wizard of OZ and realize he's a fake. He can't help them. The things they were looking for, they already had. They just needed to stir it up in them. Folks say all the time, "If I could win the lottery then I would be okay. Well, not true! Money can't make you happy. It personifies what's in you. Don't place your dreams and faith in money, but your hope is in GOD!!! God wants to give you wisdom, a new heart, and courage. He wants to bring you back home to your calling!!! Stop following rainbows, fleshly dreams, and man's opinion, and start following God's Word. He will bring you into His perfect destiny for your life!

A FATHER &
HIS SON

Occasionally, I like to share a story or a personal experience with folks that has touched my life. A while back I was visiting a very ill gentleman who was dying of cancer; I noticed sadness in his demeanor. He only had a few weeks to live, and after visiting with him it was evident that he had some unfinished business to take care of before he passed. He was a born again Christian, and was ready to go home to the Heavenly Father for eternity. But I felt there was something wrong – locked up within him. So, after reading some scripture to him and saying a prayer, I asked if there was anything else I could do or if there was anything else on his mind that he would like to talk about. With very little hesitation he began to tell me about his son. They had a disagreement that erupted into an argument and escalated into a full-fledged family feud. He went on to tell me that the two of them hadn't talked in over ten years. I asked him if he would like for me to contact his son for him, and he smiled and nodded as a tear flowed down his face. A few days later the son met me at his father's home. The two of them talked, cried, and laughed together... A few weeks later he went home to be with his Lord, in peace.

This story is close to my heart because it is very similar to my father and grandfather. When I was just a baby, my dad and granddad got into a fight about something. I say something because no one remembers what it was that they disagreed on. The two of them refused to talk for the next 15 years. After my grandfather passed away, my father stood in the funeral home and wept over his casket. But it was too late; time ran out on their relationship. When I think about some of the family feuds that people have told me about and the ridiculous reasons families fight, it breaks my heart. Time is so short. Let's not wait for our loved ones to be on their deathbed or in a casket to tell them how you feel! Put aside the past and focus on a bright future together with your loved ones! You'll be happier for it!

XV

GREEN EGGS &
HAM EVANGELISM

*S*everal years ago, a Methodist church invited be to speak at an evening revival service. That night I showed up and the tiny little church was packed. I stood at this traditional pulpit, opened my Bible, and looked up at all of these eyes staring at me. I told the congregation that I was going to preach out of the book of "Sam." All of the people thought I was going to preach out of the book of Samuel. Well, they were fooled. I reached into my folder and pulled out a Dr. Seuss book, Green Eggs and Ham. You can see how this might upset some tables in this church. I said, "Some preachers uses KJV, others use NIV, tonight I am going to preach out of the DSV (Dr. Seuss Version).

I believe that this Dr. Seuss kid's book about a furry little man named Sam-I-Am gives us an insight on how to evangelize. Let me explain. In the book Green Eggs and Ham we meet the two main characters; Sam-I-Am and an Angry Furry Man with no name that dislikes a lot of things, including Green Eggs and

Ham. The star of the book, Sam-I-Am, has a product - Green Eggs and Ham. He obviously loves to eat Green Eggs and Ham, and knows that if he can convince the Angry Furry Man to try them, he too will love them! It becomes his mission to get Angry Furry Man to try Green Eggs and Ham. So what does this have to do with evangelism? I'm glad you asked. We as Christians have a product called eternal salvation through Jesus. We have tasted the love and grace of God, and found it to be GOOD! Now we have a mission - to sell this product to a dying world! There is an angry world out there that needs to try our product. We know if they could just talk with Jesus, that they too would fall in love with Him and never turn away! Our job - our mission - is to bring our product, salvation, to a dark and angry world!

The book Green Eggs and Ham starts out with the Angry Furry Man making a statement, "That Sam-I-Am, that Sam-I-Am, I do not like that Sam-I-Am." If this was us trying to evangelize, we would stop right here. If we were going to witness to a sinner and they started the conversation with they didn't like us, we would get an attitude about it and leave. We would never go back to them, and then we would call all of our Christian brothers and tell them how mean this ungrateful man was. But what did Sam-I-Am do? He ignored the Furry Man's anger and asked this question, "Do you like Green Eggs and Ham?" He knew his mission wasn't to sell himself; he wasn't in it for a popularity contest. He was there on a mission; to get the Angry Furry Man to try Green Eggs and Ham. We need to be as persistent as Sam-I-Am when evangelizing. We are not here for a popularity contest; it's insignificant if folks like me or not! My mission is to get folks to try Jesus! Evangelizing is not about me, it's about my products - salvation, grace, and mercy!

So in the book, the Angry Furry Man tells Sam-I-Am that he wanted no part of Green Eggs and Ham. If this was most Christians, they would just leave. Not Sam-I-Am, he comes back. Watch this. It's the same product; it's just in a different package. Would you eat them in a box, with a fox, in a boat, with a goat etc.... Time and time again, Sam-I-Am comes back with the same product in a different package. Again, he's on a mission to get this man to try his product, and he won't stop until the man tastes Green Eggs and Ham. Talk about how to face rejection! Sixteen times he comes back with his product in a different package, trying to convince Angry Furry Man to eat Green Eggs and Ham.

So many times we invite folks to church and to special services, and when they don't come, we feel rejected and seldom return. How many times are you willing to go back to invite someone to church? Even if they reject the Word, even if they reject you, keep going back! Sometimes we need to be like Sam-I-Am and change the package we're bringing to them.

Remember, the product remains the same, we just change the package. The old rugged Cross may do it for some folks, but others may need Toby Mac. The message is the same; the package is just a little different. I knew a preacher who started a church in the 80's and several purple haired rockers with mohawks came to his church and got saved. The leaders wanted to start a class to teach them to cut their hair. The preacher said to leave them alone; they might have mohawk friends who need to be saved. They could minister to their friends where the church folks couldn't. I have a very good friend and spiritual son named Steve who is a biker. He preaches to other bikers in a way that I can't. The message stays the same; the package or the way that we deliver it just changes. To reach a dying world, we must be willing to be persistent with the Gospel. We must be willing to break tradition and change things up a bit every now and then.

Salvation - the world needs to try it… it's better than Green Eggs and Ham!!!

XV

THE FISH LADY & A STRANGER ON THE PHONE

*D*o you believe in God doing amazing things in our lives? Well I do, and I have experienced the supernatural time and time again. Here are a couple of stories that happened to me several years ago, and how God used a fish lady and a stranger on the other line to bring me comfort and prayer.

My Kaitie was a newborn and still in the hospital. It was the day before her first surgery, and needless to say Benita and I were a mess. I was driving home from work at a radio station heading to the hospital at Morgantown. As I was driving down the road, I began to pray to God. Then my prayer became more of me venting to God. I remember shouting, "God don't You hear me! Are You even listening to me?" The moment I said that my cell phone rang; you could imagine how freaked out I got. I almost wrecked as I ran the car to the other side of the freeway and pulled off on the road side. I looked at my cell phone and it read "no data", so I answered it with a slow "Hello." A man's voice on the other end, as shaky as mine, said "Hello, you don't know me." He quickly said, "Sir, please don't hang up." I said, "Okay." He said that he was praying and God gave him my phone number and told him to call me. He went on to ask me if I had a sick child. "Yes, I do" I said, very unsure of what was happening. He went on to ask if she had problems with her throat and voice. By this time I was in tears and pretty much beside myself. "Go on", I whispered through the lump in my throat. He said, "God says that your daughter will be healed, and you will see a day when she is singing at church." He then asked to pray with me and I obviously agreed. We talked a few minutes and hung up. I went to the hospital and told Benita what happened. She was so excited. She and I prayed together and from that point on we knew God was moving in a mighty way through our daughter.

I was sharing this story at a church in Clarksburg, WV, when a middle aged man walked up to me in tears and said "I'm Brad, the man on the other line." Wow, you gotta' be kidding me! I brought my Kaitie up to meet him. He just stood there weeping at the fact God used him to send me a message. What a great God we serve. Not only did we get a miracle of a lifetime, but God brought the stranger on the other line and I together in a church service to celebrate our miracle!

If that wasn't strange enough, we had a similar situation happen in a neighboring town of Elkins. Benita, the girls and I went to a small catch and release pond to go fishing on a Sunday afternoon. Kaitie was about three years old at this time. The lady that owned the fish pond came over where we were standing and began talking about how cute our girls were. Kaitie was extremely small for her age, and wore small Fisher Price glasses. The lady asked about her. We began to tell her about how God gave us her miracle and how God had moved through our family. She stared at Kaitie and quickly looked up and asked what her name was again. We told her and she began to cry. She went on to tell us about a prayer request at her church a few years ago. Her preacher told them about a Youth Pastor's baby that was very sick and needed a miracle. She said that God moved on her to pray for this little baby named Kaitie every night. This stranger had prayed for my daughter every night for two years.

She asked if she could hold Kaitie while we were fishing. I can still see this prayer warrior walking around that pond praising God for the miracle. This stranger praised, prayed, and sang while holding my Kaitie for about an hour.

When folks tell me that God doesn't hear prayer or listen anymore, I just smile and say, "Keep your faith. He might just be using a stranger to deliver your miracle too."

James 5:14-16 KJV

[14]*Is any sick among you? let him call for the elders of the church; and let them pray over him, anointing him with oil in the name of the Lord:* [15]*And the prayer of faith shall save the sick, and the Lord shall raise him up; and if he have committed sins, they shall be forgiven him.* [16]*Confess your faults one to another, and pray one for another, that ye may be healed. The effectual fervent prayer of a righteous man availeth much.*

A LOVE SONG
WITHOUT WORDS

*J*esus sat down, and began to eat,
When she bowed before His feet,
The tears she cried, they fell like rain,
A repentant heart, Jesus felt her pain.

She cried…
I'll sing you a love song from my heart,
I pledge that you're my world,
A new life I will start,
I'll sing to you — a love song, without words.

My story friends, is quite the same,
I know the day I came.
Some may say, they know my past,
His forgiving hand will always last.

And I cry…
I sing you a love song from my heart,
I pledge that you're my world,
A new life I will start,
I sing to you — a love song, without words.

LIGHT UP A LIFE

*O*ur Creator has placed a light in each of us,
To shine like a bright and morning star,
When this life on earth has come and gone,
The light within will still shine from afar.

During this Christmas season we reflect back to the
start,
God's sign of the love of Jesus burns brightly
within our hearts,
During days of trials, sadness becomes my fleece,
But still I hear a calm voice speak out; Jesus gives
me peace.

I feel Him working within me, blessed assurance I
now know,
I have love and peace just like a child, homeward
someday I will go,
So as we celebrate this season, it's His Joy we
receive,
The Holy Spirit will give us comfort and power:
This I truly believe.

Today as we illuminate this light as a symbol,
God's burning out the remnants of our sin,
Let us join with the saints from the past and
present,
And share God's light from within.

So holding this flame high,
We join with our brothers and sisters and say,
God, thank you for the gift of Your Son, and King,
Jesus, Happy Birthday!!!

XV

MY FRIEND R.P.

*M*any times in our lives we encounter someone who has had such an influence upon our life, that they literally help shape and define our character. Throughout my life God has placed many of these folks in my life, and to each and every one of them I am ever so thankful. In this chapter I am going to talk about a man who I met when I was just nineteen, and his life-wisdom changed my life! His name is Ralph Poling, or R.P. for short.

I got a job as a stock boy at a small country store that R.P. owned, "Poor Ralphs County Store." I was only a teenager and really knew nothing about work or life for that matter. R.P. took me in under his wing and began to pour his common sense wisdom about life into me. R.P. and I became the best of friends as I worked for him for the next eight years. During those eight years, we spent between eight to twelve hours a day together. R.P. told me to "learn everything about everything." He said, "You'll never know when you may need to use that knowledge!" So, I took the advice of R.P. and learned every trade that I could. From cutting meat, to making bows, to identifying over twenty varieties of apples, to making fruit baskets. If someone would teach me, then I learned it. I think back now about that advice. I think we all should share that same advice with our children.

R.P. was a very interesting man. He was a WWII veteran who was a POW/MIA in Romania during the war. He would periodically tell me stories about being a gunner on the B-24 plane and how his plane was shot down. One story he told was how the co-pilot saved his life after the plane was hit. Apparently, he was knocked out during the hit and his co-pilot climbed up to him and threw him out of the burning plane. He said when he landed, the local police arrested him and the other men from the B-24 crew. He told me about walking through this little town and how the local town folks came out and lined the streets as they were paraded through the town. He said they shouted curse words at them at them, and spit at them. He said even the little kids would spit at them. He was turned over to the soldiers and placed in a POW Camp. It was in the POW Camp that he met a Romanian princess that would come in to help nurse the allied soldiers. He and the princess became very close friends during his stay at the POW Camp.

This story gets very interesting from here. After the war, R.P. moved back to Philippi, WV and took over his family's store. In the 1980's he received a phone call that a Romanian princess was looking for an American soldier from WWII that she befriended in a POW Camp named Ralph Poling. The Romanian princess came to our small town of Philippi to see R.P. She stopped by his store and visited with him and they spent much time talking about the time they spent together at the WWII POW Camp. She and R.P. stayed in touch throughout the remainder of their lives.

It was thousands of stories like this one that R.P. would share with me daily. Then he would follow the story up with some good old fashion advice about life. He was very active in his church, so he also would share Biblical wisdom and different scriptures with me as well. When R.P. passed away, I can say Barbour County, WV lost a community pillar. I look forward to the day when I will see R.P. again on the other side, and together we can worship God for eternity!

Let me end this chapter with some advice. Number one - always look for folks like R.P. who have been around for a while to pour life-wisdom into your life. Soak every thing they give you into your mind and heart. Then from the advice of R.P, "Learn everything about everything, you never know when you might need to use it!"

Be blessed.

XV

A Call From Ric

I was working at a small country store and also serving as a Youth Pastor at my church, when Benita got pregnant with Hannah. Benita was working for the FBI and she was our family's "bread winner." My pay check was entertaining money we spent on movies, dinners, etc. Well, after Hannah was born, we both felt like God wanted Benita to stay at home and be a stay-at-home mother for our children. So, she quit her government job. Now, my paycheck at the store wasn't enough to pay our bills, but we both felt like her decision was the right one. So we placed our bills in the hands of God. Looking back now I see how much faith that decision took, but we serve a faithful God. For six months we lived on my pay check, while taking a twenty-five thousand dollar decrease in pay. When you added up our bills, they were close to 10 times what I was bringing home. But like I said, we serve a faithful GOD! God provided in a mighty way during those six months; we didn't only pay our bills, but we had extra! During that time our new car was paid off, we got new carpet in our home, we received a new washer and dryer, and all of our bills were paid in full.

Six months to the day, we were in church during a Sunday service. One of our church Deacons was moving, so he preached that morning and said goodbye to the congregation. After he had finished sharing, he gave an altar call and prayed with everyone. Benita and I stood before him as he walked over to us; he smiled and said a phrase that changed our lives. He said, "You both will receive a huge financial blessing this week from God." As we drove home, I remember telling Benita that I received that word and I was ready for God's blessing.

The very next day as I was at work in the country store, I received a phone call. The man's voice on the other end said, "You don't know me, but my name is Ric, and I am the General Manager for a radio corporation. I would like to offer you a job." You can't make this stuff up! I told him that I knew nothing about radio, and he said he would personally train me. He said he had met me on a few occasions as I was volunteering for the local county fair board. Now here is where the story gets cool. He said the day before he was watching TV, and God spoke to him and told him to call me up and give me a job. Ric is a man of very strong faith, and a former Church of God minister, so he knew the voice of the Lord and knew to listen to God.

I accepted the job, knowing it was from God. Ric met with me and explained to me that God was going to use him to cultivate my gifting to make money so

I might be a blessing to my family, my church, and others. Ric spent the next eight years pouring out his wisdom and knowledge of radio, sales, and faith to me. I was like a sponge, absorbing everything he taught me. With Ric, it was like God gave me my own personal professor to mentor me each day! Ric and I became more than the best of friends; he became a second father to me. Today, I owe this man more than I could repay in a lifetime! He didn't just believe in me, but he taught me how to believe in myself! As I have traveled throughout the nation sharing Ric's marketing philosophy with others, I will never forget this great man and the gift of knowledge he has given to me. Ric has since moved several hours away, but he and I will remain friends for life!!!

"Be obedient to God and He will send folks to take care of you and help watch over you!"

Benita- I love you
more now than ever!

MY BENITA &
MEAT LOAF?

*W*hat do you say about someone who is literally a part of you? I met my wife when she was in fourth grade. The night my family came to visit the church where she attended, I sat on the pew in front of her and I could see this skinny little girl glaring at me the entire service. After church, she went home and told her mother that the boy that was at church that night was the man she was going to marry when she got older! Yeah, fourth grade! My wife always knew what she wanted and most of the time she gets it!

Throughout the next few years Benita and I became very good friends, but I didn't want a steady girlfriend. She was too young for me anyway! Well, they do grow up!!! Benita starting dating when she was a freshman, but it was two years later that we became steady boyfriend and girlfriend. She was in eleventh grade and I was out of school and working. We became pre-engaged, and then engaged. The night I proposed to her, I picked her up and gave her a box of Cracker Jacks. She opened them up, and I asked her what prize she got. She said, "Well, it isn't a diamond ring…." I just about lost it; you see I had placed her ring in the box earlier that day. I watched as she opened up the tiny Cracker Jack prize package. She screamed out, "It is a diamond ring!!!" Then she looked at me somewhat confused and asked, "How did you get it in the Cracker Jack box?" I shouldn't tell you that while all of this was going on I had strategically placed a "love song" in my car's tape deck. It was a Meat Loaf song – "Two Out of Three Ain't Bad." I guess I never really listened to the words of the song! "I want you, I need you. but there ain't no way I'm ever gonna' love you, so don't be sad, two out of three ain't bad." To this day every time someone mentions Meat Loaf or one of his songs, we both laugh! On August 7, 1994, I married my school sweetheart and we started our life-journey together!

I have watched Benita grow up from a child into the mighty woman of God that she is today! She has become one of the greatest modern Worship Leaders, a musician that plays over 14 instruments, a great song writer, my Co-Pastor, the church Administrator, and the best friend that a man could ever dream of! Recently, along with all of her duties at the church and being a full time wife and mother, she went back to college and completed her bachelor's degree in Theology. Benita is more than just my wife; she is a modern day voice to the saints! When she sings, preaches or prays, the gates of Heaven rattle and the pits of Hell shakes! She has become a great mother, an amazing wife, and a True Mighty Warrior and a General in God's Army!

MARCH 11TH

*M*arch 11, 1973, my older brother William was playing with several of my other older brothers and some neighbor kids at an old coal mine above my house. The decided to make a raft from some old tree limbs and float it in a nearby pond. Now is a good time to tell you that none of the kids could swim. So they tied together the limbs with twine, and placed it into water. Two of my older brothers, Joe and William, climbed on the raft as it floated into the pond. In just a few seconds, the limbs came untied and the raft sank. Both boys, William, age ten and Joe, age nine, went under the water. Joe was closest to the bank and the boys were somehow able to pull Joe out from the water. William wasn't as fortunate. He was larger and was farther out in the water; so the boys watched their brother and friend fight for his life and drown in the pond. Losing a 10-year old son and brother is something that you never forget! I often wonder what his life would have been like if he would have made it that day. I wonder is he would have a wife and kids, if he would be in church…

Now here comes the bizarre "rest of the story." March 11, 2006, thirty-three years later to the day, I found myself at a funeral home preaching my oldest brother Lawrence's funeral. With 360 days in a year, what is the chance that one brother would die and another brother would be buried on the same date? My brother Lawrence and I were very close. He was 17 years older than I, so he was like a second father to me. I remember spending summers visiting him in Ohio. Those memories will be locked in my mind for ever. Lawrence was a Sothern Gospel music singer. He would travel around from church to church playing his guitar and singing songs he wrote. He and I would talk for hours on the phone about where God was taking us and how God was moving in our lives. Lawrence was so tender hearted; he would never hurt anyone. His life was taken from us way too young. It took several years for me to forgive those responsible for Lawrence's death. I release them and pray that they will repent before it is too late. A day will come when they will answer to God for their actions!

When we lose a loved one, sometimes we hear that we need to get over it. Well, I have come to realize that we can never get over it. Our loved ones are a part of us. But with God's help and the comforting power of the Holy Spirit, we get through it! I challenge folks to cherish the memories of their loved ones who have passed. We who have received Jesus into our hearts have the blessed assurance that we will see our loved ones again on the other side! What a great day that will be when we meet our mothers, fathers, grandparents, brothers, sisters, and friends in eternity. We will be in perfect peace and harmony without pain, sorrow, death, sickness, or disease. We will join with them in the Heavenly Choir and worship God throughout the ages!

My two brothers have started the Heavenly reunion, and there will be a day that I will be called home to join them once again! Until that day, I cherish the memories of my two big brothers, and March 11th will always be a somber day for me and my family.

Pastor Howard and Dad (Lawrence)

Pastor Howard and Mom (Pauline)

XV

THAT'S WHERE I CAME FROM

*A*s I have already shared in the book, I was born number eight of nine kids. We were always a very close family growing up. We didn't have a lot of money, but we had love for one another and back then that seemed to be enough. Let me take time and share a bit about my siblings. Lawrence was the oldest; he was the serious one of the family. He liked to joke, but only on his terms. With my practical joke personality, you can see how he and I got along. David is next; he was always strong in his faith. Growing up he was the prayer warrior of the family. Next we have Joe; he is a black belt in karate and a very good musician. William was next; he was the one taken from us when he was only ten years old. Then Carl; what can you say about my big brother Carl? He is a poster child for what a Godly servant should be! He is always serving others and seldom thinking about himself!

Now let's talk about my two sisters, Mary and Buffy. Mary is my oldest sister; she and I are very similar.

Our personalities and values are somewhat comparable. She is a cancer survivor, and we have had a lot of prayer moments together. Then Buffy; she and I are only 20-months apart in age. Although we have drifted somewhat in our adult lives, we still love each other in a special way. I'm number eight, and then six years behind me is the baby of the family, Sam. Growing up, Sam and I fought each other and played together, but I was and will always be his big brother. He can never deny me because he and I look very much alike.

My mother and father were somewhat typical West Virginia parents. My father was retired from the coal mines and suffers black lung as a result. He and I were always very close. Several of my siblings pegged me as his favorite. Because of the age gap between me and my brothers, and with my two sisters being females, growing up I really had no one my age to spend time with. I often think my dad saw that, and that's why he spent so much time with me. Growing up, when my dad would leave the house I was with him. I was daddy's boy, and I spent hours during the day with my father! Even when I became a teen and got into trouble, I always respected my dad and made sure he never knew all of the things I was into.

Recently, my dad told me that over the years he always worried about his kids, but he never worried about me. I know when others were wondering where I was heading, my dad always believed in me and he has always been very proud of me! Now my mother; I only remember being spanked one time when I was growing up (not that I didn't deserve it more)! And it was by my mom. My mother is tough as nails! She fought cancer when I was in high school and beat the odds! Time and time again, I just look at my mom in amazement of how strong emotionally, physically, and spiritually she is. As strong as she is - she is also very stubborn. I joke that the devil would never pick a fight with mom; she is too stubborn to back down!

Although my life is very different than my parent's life, I know that God blessed me with a set of parents that love me unconditionally! Mom and dad are always so proud of all of their kids and their accomplishments!

On Hacker Creek

When I share my stories with folks about the days growing up on Hacker Creek, and the interesting folks that I grew up with, sometime they say, "You're making this up." I just smile and say, "You can't make this stuff up!" Picture this, nine Swick kids living in a three bedroom house on Hacker Creek. On the hill near us lived a family with two boys nick-named Pat-Poose and Pooch. On that same road we had a Digger, Daisy, Punk, Dump, Arlie and Feeby *(fee-bee)*, Wiggles, Hoppy, Dorie *(door-ie)*, Bloomy, Idey *(eye-dee)*, and Rupert! All that we were missing was a Happy, Sleepy, and Doc! As God moves me through life, I will never forget those days on Hacker Creek. They say you can change your future, but there is one thing that you can't change and you should never forget; and that is where you came from!!! A little community called Hacker Creek, WV – that's where I came from!

CAMP CHAOS

*C*amp Chaos is what I call our first Youth Summer Camp. Our youth group began to grow from seven kids to sixty kids every week and reaching hundreds of kids throughout the tri-state area. So, we made a decision to host a Youth Summer Camp. Wow! What an experience, and what a week! Benita and I directed the camp with over 130 campers. God moved each day in a mighty way, and the devil began to attack us in every way he could. Here are just a few stories from that week at camp.

The first night, the kids began to worship God from the start of the service and the night progressed. Kids came forward at the altar call and received Christ into their hearts, and many were filled with the Holy Spirit. Now here is the start of the chaos; as kids were inside worshiping, outside another conservative church group had gathered in a candle light vigil, praying against our service because we "spoke in tongues." Yeah, the week's chaos kept growing as this group met each night to pray against our service.

And the chaos continued. During the week we had a 16-year old girl have a miscarriage (she didn't even know she was pregnant), and we had to call her mom and dad and have them take her to the hospital. She left camp and spent the rest of the week with her parents. And the chaos continued. We had a man smoking a joint break into the girl's dorm and into my wife's room. (On a side note, Benita my wife is a 3rd degree red belt in karate. Needless to say, she kicked him out of the dorm quickly.) Another Camp Counselor and I chased this guy through the woods in the rain for the next three hours, into the morning. Then we had to go the local police station and fill out a police report and return to the camp before breakfast. Needless to say, we were very tired during the morning service that day. And the chaos continued.

After the morning service, on day two, a representative from the camp facility came in and asked to meet with me. He said they had booked a local piano concert on the Wednesday night of the camp and we could not have a church service that night. So, I had to get the signed contract and show him that we had the chapel all week and explained that he would either have to join us or cancel his piano concert. And the chaos continued. During the next morning service, we had a gentleman in a suit walk in during worship and grab the microphone and try to stop the kids from singing and praising. I grabbed his arm and walked him to the side of the room and asked him what his problem was. He explained to me that he was a voice teacher and he taught voice lessons next door. He went on to tell us that our praise and worship was disturbing his flow. I explained to him that we had rented that facility for the week, so he left. I literally had to carry my signed contract with me all week.

And the chaos continued day after day! One day, they tried to move our breakfast time to 6:00 a.m.; another day they tried to close the pool. That week we had a fifteen year old run away with her nineteen year old boy friend; and another counselor and I had to go and hunt them down. Our church's worship leader came to camp one night and decided he was quitting church. A boy came to an evening service carrying a hand gun. We had adult counselors fighting with other counselors. The chaos continued all week long. But looking back, now I see that even in all of the chaos, God was still moving. We had so many kids give their lives to the Lord that week. It seemed that the more opposition came against us, God just moved more and more.

The last day of camp, after an awesome worship service, the kids came up to the altar and held hands and began to pray. I still remember standing there watching 130 kids singing "Our God Is An Awesome God." I remember thinking that even in all of the chaos, God was still moving in the hearts of those kids. God was still being exalted, and the devil was kicked down. What a testimony that whatever goes on in your life, God is still bigger! God is always in control, even in the chaos! Looking back, I wouldn't trade that week of chaos for all of the money in the world. To the 130 campers who are adults now with kids of their own; thanks for the great memories.

I Lay Down

I lay down before Your Throne,
I worship You, And You Alone.
I lift my hands and praise Your Name,
I surrender all unto Your Holy Name!

Jesus,
Jesus You're the Name above all names,
You are Holy and Anointed
And Worthy of all praise!

Jesus – I worship You
Jesus – I worship You
Jesus – I worship You
Jesus – I worship You

You are Holy and Anointed
And Worthy of all praise!

Pastor Howard Swick

ME

*W*ow, my testimony, so much to say… I have already shared about my church, my family, wife and kids, brother and sisters. Now comes the end of my book, and I get to share a bit about me. Growing up I was kind of a loner. I never fit in with my brothers and sisters real well. Actually a couple of my siblings were talking one night about our childhood, and they came to the conclusion that they didn't remember me at all when I was a kid. Most of the time I played alone when I wasn't with dad. My kid brother was six years behind me, and next to me were two sisters playing with dolls.

As I grew into a teenager, my isolation grew worse. I started developing this great jokester personality, but a wound of isolationism began to appear on my heart. I started to feel inferior to the other kids at school and my siblings. I saw everyone else, and all of the great things they could do, but I had none of those talents. So I withdrew! I spent most of my home time from sixteen to nineteen years of age in my room with no lights on, listening to music. At the age of sixteen, God called me to preach. I remember sitting on my bed and having these visions of me preaching at school and kids getting saved. At that time someone gave me a Christian rock tape, Stryper, and I loved it! This was what I was searching for. Without anyone knowing it, I began to read my Bible and pray. Then I made the mistake of reaching out to my church. I told my Pastor that I was listening to this new Christian group Stryper. He and his wife sat me down and rebuked me. They told me how evil this Christian rock was, and that I should quit listening to it. So I did! I started listening to heavy metal music and filthy rap music.

At that time I figured that Christians really didn't know what they were talking about, and that most didn't know why they believed what they believed, so I just QUIT! I decided there had to be a greater force out there, and I wasn't finding it in church. I still attended church until I turned eighteen, but mostly because I wanted to argue with the Pastor and/ or Sunday School teachers. During my junior and senior years in high school, I started studying New Age, Wicca, and Devil Worship. I was moved at the passion these followers had for their faith. I didn't see that kind of passion in the church! So I bought a Satanic Bible and began to search for answers. The funny thing is that every time I would try to run from God, He would catch me. And every time I would search for truth I would find it, but in my Holy Bible.

After I got out of school the call of God was still following me! But I kept running from it! I started using speed, smoking and drinking to find answers. I fell into a state of depression at the age of eighteen and became suicidal. I would take speed pills to get a high, then I was the life of the party. Then the high would wear off and I would drive to an old coal mine, stand on a fifty foot high wall and try to think of a reason not to jump. Each time it had to be the Spirit of God that would stop me. I would get back in the car and sometimes cry for hours. The people who were the closest to me had no idea what I was battling. Then one day God spoke to me and said, "I have called you out for a purpose. Now is the time that you need to make the decision to answer my call!" It was at that moment I realized that God has had His hand upon me from the start! It was Him that I was looking for all along. So, that day I totally committed my life to God and the call of God on my life, and it has been quite a ride ever since! I have seen miracles, signs and wonders. I have held hands and prayed with hundreds of people as they left this world and took their place in eternity. I have preached to thousands of teenagers, and God has used me to bring thousands of young people into His Kingdom! God has called me to be a husband to the greatest woman ever created, a father to two special girls, a Pastor in a great church and a Chaplain for the terminally ill. I have been everything from a store manager, a radio personality, a business executive, a corporate vice-president, and a Hospice Director. And now, I'm writing a book.

I stand amazed that God has used me, a wild child from Hacker Creek, WV, to do all of that! In conclusion let me say this, is doesn't matter who you are or where you are from, if you let Him - God will use you! The Best You is yet to come!

HOW TO RECEIVE
SALVATION

*W*e believe that Salvation is a **FREE** gift of God's grace. You can never earn it! So how do you know if you're saved? Very simple, ask yourself these two basic questions:

1. Is Jesus Christ your Savior and the Lord of your life?
2. If you were to pass today into eternity and you were standing before God, do you have the assurance of knowing that you would go to Heaven?

If your answer to either of these questions is "No", or "I don't know", please accept Jesus into your heart and life right now by praying this prayer in faith.

"Father, I know that I am a sinner and I have sinned against You and Your Word. But you

said that if I would confess my sins, that You would forgive me of ALL of my wrong doings. I believe that Jesus is Your Son, that He shed His blood and died to wash my sins away and He was raised from death and is now sitting at Your right hand. Father, I invite you to come into my life and be my Savior. Make me whole and make me new, but most of all, teach me to love, not as the world loves, but the way You love. In Jesus' name I pray, Amen."

If you prayed this prayer for the first time, please let someone know immediately. And most of all get connected to a **local church!**

God bless!

Pastor Howard

About The Author

 Pastor Howard was born and raised in a little community called Hacker's Creek, about four miles from the small Civil War town of Philippi, WV. He was number eight of nine children, and the son of a retired coal miner. Like many families of Appalachia, the Swick family was very poor, and with nine kids to feed there wasn't a lot of money to spare. So like other small town families, they lived off the land with several gardens, growing a lot of what they ate.

"We were raised poor, but until we grew up we didn't know just how poor we were. Mom and dad always made sure that there was food on the table and clothes on our backs. We fought like all families, but God was always respected in our home and we were all taught to honor Him in all that we do! " Pastor H

When Howard was just a few months old, his parents Lawrence and Pauline joined with a Pastor named Pete Parsons. Together with a few other families, they started one of the first Pentecostal churches in Barbour County (Ford Run Pentecostal Church). The Swick family moved from Pentecostal to Southern Baptist for about six years, and then joined the Nazarene Church when Howard was in seventh grade. It was in the Nazarene Church that Howard became curious about God's Divine nature. At the age of sixteen, he began to have dreams about preaching and praying for his peers.

"At the age of sixteen God called me to preach, but like many others I was afraid to answer the call. It seemed that no one in my church, including three different Pastors and many Sunday School teachers, could see the call to preach on my life. So I just ran from it! I spent about six more years running from God and the call to preach... But during that time it seemed like I always had something to say about God and His Love. I read my Bible almost every night, studied the scriptures, and even prayed, but the dreams of preaching just kept recurring...."
Pastor H

It was in the Nazarene Church that Howard met his future wife, Benita. In 1994 the two were married in the church they met and grew up in. It was in March of 1995 Howard and Benita left the Nazarene Church and started attending a somewhat new Charismatic church in the same county called Haven of Hope Church.

In the fall of 1995 Pastor Howard along with his wife, Pastor Benita, established the Living Stones Youth Ministry at Haven of Hope. Over the past years the Swicks have reached young people with a contemporary sound and the SOLID WORD!!! They taught young people to experience life with a foundation in Jesus Christ, that He loves them, gave His life for them, and that He has an exciting destiny for their lives. In a town of about 4000 people, the Swicks hosted God-centered youth functions with about 400 youths attending. Over the years, the Swicks have literally reached thousands of youth without comprising God's Word!

"Sometimes the building just couldn't hold all of the kids that would attend our youth services; I would just sit back and wonder where they were all coming from… One time during a youth service we had about 100 kids answer an altar call for salvation (about 1/3 of the congregation)." Pastor H

Although the Swicks came from a traditional mainstream church, they never really fit in. It was like someone tried to put a square peg into a round hole. At this new Charismatic church, the Swicks found the spirituality they were searching for. After several years of Youth Ministry, in September 2003 God moved them to a Senior Pastor position at their church. Now as Senior Pastors they are as cutting edge as ever… preaching, teaching, and sharing the Good News of God with anyone and everyone they come in contact with.

"It's funny how God works. Benita and I had just gotten back from North Carolina where we had preached a youth revival. On the way home we said that we both loved evangelism, and if God never called us to Pastor a local church and just had us evangelizing, then that would be ok with us. The very next month we assumed the role as Senior Pastor of our church." Pastor H

Pastor Howard is known for preaching a modern, cutting edge, "on-fire" Word of God. He has preached revivals throughout North Central WV, Southern Pennsylvania, Maryland, and as far away as North Carolina. As a Senior Pastor, he has crossed denominational barriers and preached at Methodist, Baptist, Nazarene, Pentecostal, and other Independent Churches.

Pastor Howard also serves as a Hospice Chaplain, where he has been used by God to bring peace through God's Word into homes of the terminally ill throughout WV and Southwestern PA. He has spoken at many forums locally, regional, statewide, and nationally on the spiritual aspects of end of life care.

From prison ministry, hospice chaplaincy, youth ministry, to homeless ministry, Pastor Howard has developed a unique style to share God's love with the hurt and lost. If it's in a church, night clubs, or even crack houses; Pastor Howard shares God's love with all who will listen.

"People just want to be loved on and accepted! That is really what ministry is all about; loving on folks! I have shared God's love – in a loving way – with alcoholics, drug addicts, Atheists, homosexuals, Wiccans, Muslims, and Buddhists... and each time it's the love of God that grabs them, not condemnation!" Pastor H

Contact Information

Thank you for reading XV! If you would like to order more books or contact Pastor Howard, please use the contact information below:

Pastor Howard Swick
PO Box 886
Philippi, WV 26416
Phone - 304-823-3428
hswick@hospicecarecorp.org

For more information about Haven of Hope Worship Center, please visit our website at:

http://www.havenofhopewv.com/